WITCH

A Tradition Renewed

In Memory of Robert Cochrane

And to Doreen, Jane, Bill,
Mike, Peter, Ann, Dave
and The Roebuck,
And Valerie for all her help.

WITCHCRAFT

A Tradition Renewed

DOREEN VALIENTE
& EVAN JOHN JONES

PHOENIX PUBLISHING INC.

This edition printed 1990

PHOENIX PUBLISHING INC.
Portal Way
P.O. Box 10
Custer, Washington USA 98240

ISBN 0-919345-61-1

Cover design by Rick Testa

Printed in the U.S.A.

Contents

Preface by Doreen Valiente   7
Introduction   15

I Rudiments of the Craft   21
  1 The Faith   23
  2 The Nature of the Rites   47
    History and Myth   52

II The Coven   69
  1 The Coven   71
    The Lady   71
    North   72
    South   72
    East   72
    West   73
    The Membership   73
    The Initiate   74
    The Man in Black   76
    The Summoner   77
  2 Coven Oaths   79
    The Initiation Oath   79
    The Oath of Full Membership   81
    The Oath of Office   83
    The Oath for the Lady   87

III Tools and Regalia   93
  1 The Working Tools   95
    The Knife   96
    The Cord   99
    The Stang   102
    Consecrating the Tools   107

2 The Coven Regalia   110
      The Cup   110
      The Coven Knife   113
      The Coven Stangs   116
      Shodding with Iron   121
      The Besom   121
      The Coven Sword   126
      The Cauldron   130
      The Skull   134

IV The Rituals   147
1 Beginning the Rituals   149
      Casting the Circle   150
      Dedication of the Cakes and Wine   154
2 The Four Great Sabbats   158
      Fasting and Purification   160
      The Royal Cairn   165
      Candlemas (2 February)   170
      May Eve (30 April)   176
      Lammas (1 August)   179
      Hallowe'en (31 October)   183
      The Rite of Handfasting   188

Appendix: a List of Sacred Woods and Trees   191
Bibliography   195
Index   199

Preface

by Doreen Valiente

This is a deeper and more serious book about witchcraft than most of the books on this subject on sale today. In fact, some readers, accustomed to a less profound view of the Old Religion, may find it disturbing. It is indeed unlike the rather airy-fairy view of 'Wicca' which has become prevalent today, with its merry ring-dances in the nude and its insistence on a bland attitude of universal optimism and love towards all. This is the view which was promulgated by Gerald Gardner from the 1950s onwards, and continued by Alex Sanders. There is no doubt that 'Wicca' has brought much enjoyment and enlightenment to many people; but there is an older witchcraft, and it is the latter that this book is about.

From those who are disturbed by some of its contents, I ask only calm consideration and a recollection of the text quoted by Margaret Murray on the title page of her famous book *The God of the Witches*: 'Look unto the rock whence ye are hewn, and to the hole of the pit whence ye are digged.' The roots of genuine witchcraft are very ancient. They go down into the deep places of human consciousness and into the prehistory of human society. Hence those roots are of necessity primitive.

I have known the author of this book, Evan John Jones, since he and I both belonged to the coven headed by Robert Cochrane in the 1960s. I have described some of the workings of this coven in my recent book *The Rebirth of Witchcraft*. Robert Cochrane was a remarkable young man, whose fame has lived on after his tragic and premature death in 1966. He claimed to be a genuine hereditary witch, drawing his teachings from a long and secret tradition. To what extent this is true, we shall probably never know. I have described my experience with his coven in my book mentioned above. As may be seen from that account, some of it was rather equivocal. However, there is one thing I know for certain. Robert Cochrane 'had something'. Call it magical power, charisma or what you will. He may have been devious; but he was no charlatan.

Very little of the workings and beliefs of Robert Cochrane's coven has penetrated to the outside world, and what has been heard has usually been garbled. However, I am told that there are a few people in the United States who have been working along his lines, using as their basis some old letters of his. Some of his old coven members in Britain also have attempted to continue his tradition. Of these, Evan John Jones is one.

However, he makes no claim that he has published the rituals used by Robert Cochrane. Indeed, it would not be possible for him to do so; because, as I remember them, most of Cochrane's rituals were spontaneous and shamanistic. He did not work from a set 'Book of Shadows', previously written down, but from a traditional way of doing things, upon which improvised rituals could be based. It is this which has been the inspiration for this book.

My task in helping to produce this book has been to edit John's manuscript, to rearrange its contents and here and there to add what I felt were some points of interest. I have also put some of his incantations into verse. However, the ideas and rituals in this book are mainly his. I have been glad to help it find publication, because I feel that it is an important book and unlike any other which has appeared on this subject. In fact, it is the only book I know of which is devoted entirely to traditional witchcraft, as opposed to more modern versions of the Old Religion.

Nevertheless, as the author admits, it is a re-creation of the old ways. In these present times, it cannot be anything else, because so much was lost in the days when witchcraft was actually a criminal offence. We often forget that those days ended only in 1951, when the last of the Witchcraft Acts was repealed.

Even after they had stopped actually hanging and

burning us, the authorities of Church and state continued a determined onslaught against the survival of the old pagan craft. Indeed, this still continues today. Every now and again we read of some fundamentalist Christian demand that a lecture be banned or a bookshop closed, in defiance of the right of freedom of information in a free society. But even more insidious was the social pressure on the lower classes to conform; not to offend the squire, or you wouldn't be able to get a job; to be a regular church-goer or chapel-goer, or you would be marked as a dubious character in some small village community. It was a crime to be 'different' from the norm which somebody else had decided for you – rather like those unfortunate schoolchildren in Wales who used to have a wooden label hung round their necks as a punishment for speaking in Welsh. And, of course, prison was still available, up to 1951, as a weapon against anyone publicly claiming to be a witch.

In these circumstances, it is really surprising that so much of the old beliefs and traditions has endured. The reason is that their roots are so deep that they have been almost impossible to eradicate; and also, that they have survived by changing their form and becoming folk customs and 'superstitions', where they were once religion and magic.

For instance, May Eve, Midsummer and Hallowe'en have never ceased to be regarded as magical nights. In fact, Hallowe'en is so much more celebrated than it used to be that we have begun to be able to buy Hallowe'en greetings cards. At the same time, Christian fundamentalists have issued leaflets denouncing its celebration and claiming that it is a pagan festival. They are quite right, of course. It is a pagan festival – and so are Christmas and Easter, if traced to their real origins. Hallowe'en is the old Celtic Eve of Samhain, one of the four Fire Festivals of the pagan year, celebrated by our ancestors from time immemorial, which became the 'Great Sabbats' of the witches. This fact in itself goes to show that witchcraft is really the remains of an ancient pre-Christian religion, and not merely superstition or 'devil-worship'.

At the present time, many Christian fundamentalists are

expending a great deal of energy in telling the world that witches, in common with most other students of the occult, are really followers of 'Satan' – even when witches deny that they believe in Satan! In this connection, I think we need to recall some wise words of that famous nineteenth-century occultist Eliphas Levi: 'He who affirms the devil, creates or makes the devil.'

In other words, by constantly telling us that there is a great power of evil, personified as Satan, which people can invoke and serve for reward, these good Christians are unwittingly creating the very concept that they denounce. To put it in the words used by occultists, they are creating upon the astral plane a huge thought-form. But this monstrosity is nothing but a mock-up, like the frightful 'demons' created in some film studio for a horror movie. It is time that we demolished it and threw the remains onto the rubbish-heap of human thought.

The powers invoked in the rituals in this book go back to the dawn of time, to the primeval Mother Goddess and the Horned God of the painted caves. Call her Mother Nature, Gaia, the Magna Mater, Mother Earth or what you will. She is, if you like, the Intelligence behind Nature, which is, as it originally was, conceived of as feminine. Her son and consort is the old Horned One whom our primitive ancestors depicted on the walls of their cave-sanctuaries. He too has many names, perhaps most happily the merry, leaping Pan who played his pipes to the witches of Thessaly. Ancient Britain knew him as Cernunnos, a deity of whom a surprising number of representations have survived, though usually of a crude and simple nature – which may be why they have endured, where a more sophisticated work of art would have been destroyed at the coming of the Christian era.

The turning wheel of the year and the celebration of the four Great Sabbats which mark it bring us closer into association with the powers of nature, epitomized in these rituals by the sowing and reaping of the grain. Strangely enough, John was quite unaware, until I told him, that the central act of the pre-Christian Mysteries of Eleusis consisted of showing to the initiates a newly reaped ear of corn. I did not tell him this until after I had read his manuscript and seen the significance he gives to this in his rituals.

Much of John's writing has been inspirational in this way. I can testify to the fact that he has no great library of books. He feels that true religion (like true magic) is a highly personal thing, which could be expressed as a 'pact', a personal relationship between a human being and what they are able to feel, as a result of meditation or kinship with nature, as the powers behind and within nature.

He has not glossed over the primitive beginnings of the Old Religion, with its relationship with the old ideas of divine kingship and the sacrificial rites involved therewith. Hence my remark at the commencement of this preface that some people might find this book disturbing. Nevertheless, it describes also the way in which these primitive beginnings have evolved into something higher.

People today are at last beginning to realize the consequences of becoming what Dion Fortune called 'orphaned of the Great Mother'. We are beginning to look at what has happened and is happening to our planet. It has at last registered upon us that whatever utopias are built upon politicians' promises, if the planet itself is ruined such promises can be nothing but wind-blown dust. Our fate is bound up with that of Mother Earth, whose children we are. Hence the emergence of what has come to be called 'Green politics'.

This, in my opinion, is another indication of the oncoming of the Aquarian Age. It is the time when we must understand and use the past in order to build upon it for the future. The Old Religion must look forward also, and continue its evolution. If it does so, it can play a vital role in the New Age. Indeed, paganism in various forms is already beginning to do this.

I must ask those who find this book disturbing, for reasons other than those I have mentioned above, to consider this aspect of the matter. There will certainly be those who will condemn John and myself for 'saying too much', 'giving away secrets' and so on. I respect their feelings on this subject, and so, I am sure, does John. However, I feel that we have to recognize the changing times, and be ready if necessary to change with them.

We are at an important turning-point in human history: the changeover from the Age of Pisces to the Age of Aquarius. Those of us who have preserved the knowledge that is known as 'occult', a word meaning simply 'hidden', now need to make use of that knowledge in a constructive way. Moreover, we have to make a stand against ignorance and bigotry, and for the recognition of our old faith as a legitimate religion.

Secrecy was in the past our means of self-defence against persecution. It was because of the tradition of secrecy that the Old Religion survived. Those who ventured to study the occult had constantly to keep in mind the traditional Four Powers of the Magus: to know, to dare, to will and to be silent. Babblers and boasters were likely to achieve very little – except to bring themselves to the notice of the witch-hunters. We are still taught that talking about magical operations weakens their power, apart from any other considerations. Even today, one of the first things any serious occultist has to learn is discretion.

We need, therefore, to avoid the extremes of either excessive secrecy or excessive publicity. In this book, I think John has tried to do that. While making it clear that there are certain things which are kept in reserve, he has shown a side of witchcraft different from anything that has been published before, to my knowledge; but at the same time we make no claim that this is the only way. On the contrary, there are many covens today which have their own way of doing things, derived either from Gerald Gardner, Alex Sanders, Zsuzsanna Budapest, Starhawk or some other source. We intend no disparagement of them. As I have said previously, in my recent book *The Rebirth of Witchcraft*, the things which unite us are very much bigger and more important than the things which divide us. Some of us will have no objection to publicity; others will prefer to remain secret. Provided that what we do is sincere and constructive, we can all live and work together with mutual respect, as children of the Great Mother and followers of the Old Gods.

In spite of the many books which have been written on the subject in recent years, most people still seem to regard witchcraft as being mainly a matter of casting spells or gaining psychic powers. They find it difficult to regard it as being a religious faith. Nevertheless, this definition has always been there, in what Margaret Murray called 'Operative Witchcraft and Ritual Witchcraft'. To her, Operative Witchcraft was a matter of charms and spells, while Ritual Witchcraft was the system of religious beliefs and ritual which she regarded as 'the ancient religion of Western Europe'. (See *The Witch Cult in Western Europe* by Margaret Alice Murray). We are beginning to find out a great deal more about the powers of the human mind than we ever did before. However, we still know very little – much less, I suspect, than our ancestors did.

One of the first things I was taught by Gerald Gardner, the witch who initiated me, was that magical powers were latent in everyone. They were the natural though mysterious powers of the inner mind. What witchcraft did, he told me, was to provide the atmosphere in which those powers could manifest. From experience, I believe this to be true. May this book help those who seek, to find the magic within themselves and nature.

Doreen Valiente

Introduction

In writing this book, I am putting down some twenty years of thoughts and feelings; twenty years of searching for something with a spiritual meaning that for me transcends the orthodox faiths. To me, what is written here answers in part what I have been searching for.

At no time do I make the claim that this is of an old tradition that has been handed down to me through my family. Rather, it is a combination of old and new. There are things that were taught to me by one who was of the old witch tradition. There are others learnt from a very knowledgeable and scholarly author and witch. Finally, there are those things which have come through my own thoughts and workings. But the inspiration for all of this comes from an unpublished manuscript of another old friend – and from whatever gave me the feeling that this was something I had to do.

The first contact I ever had with the Craft of the Wise was in the early sixties, a time when occultism and witchcraft in particular exploded into the public's awareness through the more sensational press. It was an interesting time, a time of excitement, flux, when anything seemed possible. In my case, this was a time of change and involvement. Life seemed to open up. It seemed as if new people, new faces and ideas flowed through the very air itself. It gave one the feeling of trying to grab a handful of water: you couldn't hold it, yet it left your palm damp. Something was there, but it was a case of trying to find it and hold on to it.

One concept was learned, but behind that was another hidden mystery. The lifting of one veil led to the finding of yet another. At the same time, one was left knowing that

15

behind all these veils was an inner core, a hidden truth that only the very select few would ever find. I have yet to reach that stage – if I ever do. But the sureness of its being there, and the knowing that it is, can be reward enough in itself.

From the first meeting, I learned one thing about the Old Faith. It was the feeling of belonging and involvement. I knew that people came and went within the group. I knew that we worked with others of a like mind. But all the time this was going on, there was a hard core of us who seemed to hang together.

From these people I learnt the secret of 'being', in the full sense of the word. Being part of something. Being able to draw on others for help and support. Being able to give of myself to others. Being able to commit myself to a different lifestyle, a different philosophy – one that made me look at myself in relation to others, and change myself to the extent wherein I became as one with the whole and they in turn were part of me; a comradeship within the circle.

However, for reasons that are private and personal and best left out of these pages, things began to go wrong for our group. The blame can be laid firmly at the door of one person only, who was an intrusion into our group that would have been best left out. But the Fates decreed otherwise; and Robert Cochrane, our leader, who had preached to us 'not to monkey with the buzz-saw', got cut himself. This led to the painful break-up of his marriage and his eventual suicide.

Even after his death and the breaking-up of the group, his workings and ideas still influence people who never even met him and who know of his workings only through the letters he left. Even today in America there are groups trying to rebuild what we had, through those letters.

From contact with some of these people, I have found out a few of the myths and legends which have attached themselves to his name and memory. Rumour has it that our leader, Robert Cochrane, died in the circle. This is not true. Though there was some religious element in his death, it was not as dramatic as this. I know, because I was with him on the eve of his dying. I still have the tie he left behind when he returned home that night. That and what we talked about will be with me for the rest of my life.

Because I was newly married and living in London, I suppose we fell away from each other a bit. But on this particular Sunday, Robert Cochrane came up from his home to see us and two other group members. The three of us had a meal afterwards, and round about seven o'clock in the evening he went home. One of the things that stuck in my mind was the way in which he had said that 'his future was in the lap of the Goddess'. The other thing he stressed was that he would be with us for an important date, but not in body, and that 'he would be hunting from the Other Side'. Not long after saying this he left.

Repeated telephone calls on the Monday night got no answer; so I phoned another friend to go round to Cochrane's place and check if he was there. We learned that he had been found in the garden by the next-door neighbours at about four in the morning and that he was in hospital. He had eaten the foliage of a belladonna plant (deadly nightshade). Three days later he died.

One other thing that has stayed with me to this day, never to be forgotten or forgiven, is the fact that during the police inquiry afterwards some people denied that they had ever worked with him. They had only been along to observe, they said.

For me personally, I had lost a friend who was more like a brother to me. When Robert Cochrane died, something of myself died as well. For a while I felt betrayed. I had given so much of my trust, only to lose it in his dying. Yet after a while, and after we had moved to Brighton, the feeling that he was still around was very strong. At certain times his presence could be felt; and not long after, I had the feeling that I should return to one of our old working sites in Sussex. Each year for the past twenty years, two of us have been making the trip up to that site. Each summer, arthritis, ill-health and bad weather have never stopped us. But now the time has come to stop.

On the nineteenth anniversary of Robert Cochrane's death, we were given right out of the blue a green candle, decorated with a pattern of acorns and oak leaves. This was taken to the site and lit at the foot of the oak tree where we once held a ritual. On the twentieth anniversary, the same candle and one other from America were taken there and lit for the final time. They were buried by the tree, as this was the last time of going. Instinct tells me that whatever was there in that place is now over and done with and that it is time to permit the site to return to its loneliness. It has served its purpose, and now is the time to let go. As one door closes, another one opens.

Looking back on the past, one has the feeling that something was started but never finished. I know that Robert Cochrane's ambition was to gather in as many strands of the Old Faith as he could, and then represent them as a cohesive whole. Whether or not he would have been able to do this, we will never know. All that we do know is that the little he left still has an impact upon minds and still makes people want to explore the path we once trod. To this end, I have written what I have. I make no claim that all of it is his. Far from it; but the basic roots came from what he taught me. Combined with what I am doing now, the rites as practised work and work well. What more can you ask of a ritual than that?

Before reading any further, it should be borne in mind that, even though the four major rituals have been written with a full coven of thirteen in mind, there is no earthly reason why a single person or a smaller group should not perform them in full. In all the rites, the meanings, philosophy and ideas expressed within the concepts have been made clear. Any person wishing to follow them takes the basic idea and adapts it to suit the circumstances.

I suppose the only thing that is mandatory is the dedication of the cakes and wine. As such, a male–female partnership can do this but not a single person. I have in the past at some time or other kept every one of these festivals on my own, both indoors and outside. In the case of Candlemas, for instance, a single person can set up their own stang as an altar (what this means will be explained later). They can plant a single seed in a pot placed at the foot of it, and then raise a glass of wine in honour of the Goddess. A working couple could do the same, modifying the rite so that it suits their circumstances.

The one thing that has to be borne in mind is that the coven is a gathering of like-minded people, joining together in a formal or ceremonial act of worship four times a year. These gatherings are called Sabbats. In the monthly rituals or Esbats, usually a small group or even a couple will get together and do their own thing, outside the main coven gatherings. In ninety-nine cases out of a hundred, the meetings in both group or coven sense are an act of worship and not a working magical rite. By the latter, I mean when the gathering has come together to work a specific magical rite with a specific magical end in mind, and for no other purpose. In this case, the Dance of the Mill will be trodden widdershins (anti-clockwise) instead of deosil (clockwise/sunwise), the one being a magical act and the other an act of worship.

It is in these acts of worship that the true relationship of the individual to the Craft or Faith is bonded; because by working in either a small group or a full coven, any person is still an individual looking for something that fills an individual need. Perhaps those needs would be better filled by that person's working on their own, or with a like-minded partner, rather than being part of a formal grouping.

By taking the concept of each of the four major rituals and adapting them to suit, it is possible to keep them in a highly individual way, without losing any of the impact or satisfaction that comes with keeping them. After all, words are only the vehicle of the concept, and one's own words can represent and serve the concept just as well as the words used in the rites of any full coven. The fact that a person is not a member of any coven or has never been initiated into any coven should never hold anyone back from worshipping the Old Gods and the Goddess, should they feel the call to do so. It means that they have to find their own path, a harder but in some ways more satisfying means of gaining the wisdom. All, but all of us, start off knowing nothing and spend the rest of our lives learning to find our own way to serve the Power we call the Goddess and the Old Gods.

I   Rudiments of the Craft

1   The Faith

When people talk about the Old Faith, it raises the
question of just what they mean by this. Traditionally, 'the
Old Faith' refers to the worship of the Mother Goddess in
all her aspects; through her, the Horned God or Horned
Child as symbolized by the stang, a forked or horned staff
(see p.102). Also, the forces of nature in all its guises, even
though these are sometimes red in tooth and claw; the old
birth, death and resurrection cycle within the framework
of society; an acceptance of the not-understood forces
talked about as 'natural magic'; and the ability to
understand that, behind the veil between the known and
the unknown worlds of the natural and supernatural,
there are powers which were once the birthright of
humanity, later to be lost in our so-called advance of
material civilization.

Not that there is anything wrong with a material
civilization, providing of course that there is a spiritual
advancement at the same time. But human nature being
what it is, this unfortunately did not happen. In the search
for power over others, instead of being spiritually the
servants of humanity, the priesthood became the masters.
No longer did the servants of the gods serve the
community. They tithed, taxed and controlled it. The
gods, and later the one God, could be approached only
through the ministers of that faith. The blessings of God
could be withheld or granted by the hierarchy.

Having the power of these sanctions was not a bad
thing, providing they were used as a check against the
excesses of the secular powers. But when they were used
to enforce ecclesiastical rights and the imposition of taxes
by putting the immortal soul of an offender in jeopardy,

they became a bad thing. What was freely given in the past had now to be paid for in fear and conformity.

The rise of the patriarchal gods to pre-eminence in the city-state pantheon and later the state pantheon was always balanced with that of the corresponding female deities. Even when Christianity became the faith of the Roman Imperium and beyond, the need for a female aspect of the godhead led to the elevation of Mary the mother of Christ as the interceder between God and humanity and partially restored the concept of a Goddess, providing of course that this was still within the framework of Christian orthodoxy. In many ways, Mary took on some of the aspects of the Magna Mater, most certainly in the Christianized Grail Mysteries that appeared to have pervaded British folklore and mythos.

Today, now that to be a non-Christian is to a certain degree acceptable within society, the concept of the Goddess and the Horned God or Horned Child as deities worthy of worship no longer has to be hidden by her followers.

Perhaps unfortunately, many aspects of the faith of the Goddess were lost to humanity with the establishment of the Christian faith with all its schisms. There are hints in classical literature of the Goddess in many of her varied forms; but the strongest hints of all concerning her worship are to be found in the stronghold of her following, the countryside. Being a goddess of farm, field and woodland, many of the old country customs relate to her worship. Because she is part and parcel of nature's way, the quarterly cycles of nature are under her sway. Mirrored in the seasons are found the ages of human life: youth, maturity, old age and finally death and the rebirth with the spring planting.

Yet it was not just a simple rustic faith. Behind the simplicity of it all was a deeper faith that called for a greater understanding than blind acceptance. There was an instinctive understanding that people, collectively and individually, could not stand apart from their environ-ment. They were an intrinsic part of it.

This showed in the gradual acceptance of a totemistic animal as the guardian spirit of the tribe, group or clan.

The relationship of human beings to divinity was moulded and governed by their surroundings. The world they dwelt in was filled with influences or spirits, both good and evil, that had to be dealt with. The spirit of evil or harm had to be contained or driven out by the forces of good.

As the child is protected by the mother, so primitive people visualized the benevolent side of divinity as a stern but caring mother figure, who had to be placated by certain acts. To do wrong against her laws would bring retribution. To follow her laws would bring about her aid. Gradually a code of behaviour would be formed, and within this code the wisdom of the elders would be used to help interpret it for the generations to follow.

Today, many of the things that our ancestors used to practise and pray for are no longer relevant to our life-style. Within an artificially created system of living, we as individuals no longer have to placate the Mother in the form of the Corn Goddess for our bread. We just nip down to the supermarket and buy a loaf. This may sound as if there is a case for declaring the Goddess redundant. Not so: today more than ever people need a faith to guide them, a faith that will lead them forward and match their spiritual awareness to their material advancement. Today, even more, humanity needs a rekindling of the spirit that saw the founding of the world's great religions.

To some, the answer is to try to turn the clock back. However, fundamentalism is not the answer, nor is sectarianism. Couple fundamentalism or sectarianism with modern technology, and where men died in their hundreds for their faith, they may now die in their thousands. Blind faith can and does destroy the message that all the great faiths teach; compassion, understanding and, above all, humanity.

To say 'My God is not your God' is to belittle the Divine Spirit, trying to put a finite limit on the infinity of God. To reject the idea that there is Something to answer to, and to render an account of our life to, beyond this existence, is to break the bonds of any form of moral restraint. Man is no longer bound by his duties to others. They have in fact become his prey to use, manipulate and pillage. The only things that hold him in check are man-made laws administered in the name of God and State.

Until the Divine Spirit that created this universe is ready once more to send a messenger to point the way to the next stage in humanity's spiritual development and awareness, I must seek my own salvation in my own way and in my own form. I, like many others, have turned to the past to find the Goddess. If I make mistakes, they are *my* mistakes, not something foisted on me by others. I search for my own way to find the Godhead, knowing that the Godhead will in turn serve me by granting me a greater awareness of the mystery that is life.

In the words of the author Bill Gray's Sangreal Prayer, which was given to me by him to use in my rites:

Beloved Bloodmother of my especial breed,
Welcome me at this moment with your willing womb.
Let me learn to live in love with all you are,
So my seeking spirit serves the Sangreal.

The concept of the Holy Grail, although Christianized into the vessel which contained the wine of the Last Supper, dates back to pagan times. The old Norman-French word for it was 'San Greal' or 'Holy Grail', but this can also be translated as 'Sang Real' or 'Royal Blood'. With this usage, it refers to the Blood Royal, in the sense of the Divine Sacrificial King dying for his people. Used in this book as a prayer, it refers to the mystic 'blood-line' of the priestess who is drawn to the Craft because it is 'in the blood'.

When someone says to me, 'My Granny brought me into the Craft and taught me all I know,' it is a bit like saying, 'I've started a new line of flint knives in my cutler's shop.' The first question I always ask is, 'Surely you've got beyond that?'

Not that I am saying that what Granny taught was wrong. On the contrary, everyone must have a baseline to work from. Because of the nature of the worship of the Goddess, and because for centuries it was almost lost and destroyed as a living faith, it is not bound by aeons of hallowed tradition. It is not caught up in a liturgy of its own, and one that has singularly failed to adapt to modern thought and aspirations.

Before the coming of Christianity, worship of the Goddess in her many different forms had gradually reached the stage at which pomp and ceremony had taken over from meaning. In short, it had become fossilized. Today, thanks to that suppression, the worship of the Goddess and the gods of the high and lonely places is untrammelled by tradition and free. Anyone who decides to follow her ways learns the basic concepts and rites and then explores from there.

Because of the sheer openness of the concept, the Goddess once again is multi-faceted, and each one of these faces is valid in its own right to the worshipper. No one should say, 'What I have is the only genuine tradition. What you have is wrong.' To say this is to deny the universal nature of the Goddess and try to bind her to your own image of what you think she should be. To find the Goddess, one must explore the very fabric of life itself, because, being the Goddess of life, she is still found within life. No one – but no one – holds any great secret, only the workings and rites of their particular group or coven.

By tradition, entry into any occult order is by initiation. In the Craft, this initiation period usually lasts for a year and a day. While agreeing in principle with this system, there are always the exceptions to the procedure. In many cases people cannot find a group or coven to join, or the contacts they have with the occult do not practise the sort of thing that they as individuals want to do. So where do they go from there?

If they have a few friends of a like mind, they get together and talk over what they will look for in their workings. They read, study and gradually build up a store of knowledge from which they can form a basis on which to build their own rites. If a person is of serious intent, one night they can go out at midnight of the full moon and make their own pledge to the Goddess and the Old Gods in truth, honesty and sincerity. This sort of pledge has as much validity as any formal oath sworn to any group.

To be a member of a group is a nice thing, providing you remember that any group is nothing more than a number of like-minded people who gather together to work or worship in a certain way. Another thing to remember at this stage is that certain groups have systems of degrees of advancement. So you work through a set course and at the end of it you get a degree of initiation. Very nice too; but this degree doesn't mean a damned thing outside that group. In fact, many times it means the exact opposite, a case of 'Oh, yeah – and so what?'

The tradition that Robert Cochrane worked, and which to a certain extent I am working, never made use of any such thing. You served an apprenticeship and then were sworn in as a full member, and that was that. If people want a system of degrees, very well; but it still does not make you any better or more advanced than anyone else. It just means that you like being in a hierarchical system.

The trouble is that after a while the leaders of such a group tend to develop the idea that their way is the only way. Everyone else is wrong except them. In most groups in which this has occurred, the rites seem sterile and have no meaning. Instead of advancement, there is a feeling of being hedged in and shut off from what others are thinking and developing.

In this book, I have laid out the coven and clan system. The rites and the thinking behind them are not a great secret, nor are they all that original. If the reader wishes to build up a system akin to ours, using what is in here as a basis, by all means do so. These pages are most certainly not the be-all and end-all of the Craft. Far from it; these rites are our way of paying homage to the Goddess and worshipping her in the way we want to.

From this stage on, things have to be taken as an act of faith. Many of the things stated here are unproven and unprovable and have to be taken at face value in the belief that they are true. Within the universe there is a creative force or power, call it God or the Goddess or what-have-you, but it is there. It created out of chaos the order of the universe as we know it. Within this order came creation of life in all its varied forms, including humanity. Of all these life forms, only human beings were given that little extra spark of divinity that made them the thinking, reasoning entities which they are now.

The other power which was given to humanity by the Divine spirit was the ability to advance from the near-animal state to the stage at which the soul is as one and equal with the Godhead itself. No longer is the soul an individual thing expressed as a person. The soul or the small part of the Godhead returns to its place of origin and is reabsorbed into the divine spiritual mass or the Body of God. Thus the Godhead re-creates itself in full, with all the small fragments of itself which were used to seed the earth under the name of the human race.

To be able fully to comprehend and understand the magnitude of the Godhead is downright impossible. Most of us at the best see only one facet of divinity. The very occasional person may see more than one facet and in doing so is stamped with the mark of the Godhead. Such persons stand apart from the rest of humanity and seem no longer governed by the same feelings and emotions as the rest of us. They are like a finger pointing to our conscience and reminding us that there is more to life than our own desires and whims. Their message is never a comfortable one to listen to, because it reminds us that we have duties and debts beyond those we think we owe ourselves.

Because of the impossibility of visualizing the whole Godhead as a single entity with full comprehension and understanding, we have to reduce the concept to a form that we can understand and mentally handle. In my case, the Godhead is in the form of the Magna Mater – the Great Mother, goddess of infinite understanding and infinite compassion for her wayward child, me.

While the body as a vehicle of this existence is limited to one life span, the soul or spirit that is the immortal essence of the person survives death, only to be reborn again. Each and every one of us has to go through this cycle of birth, death and rebirth, not once but many times. Each time we are reborn, we have to fulfil a fate that is predetermined by our past existence. The fate we created in one life we have to live out in another. But at the same time we must also learn a lesson, if we have gained sufficient wisdom to learn from the past.

These lessons are the things that take us one step at a

time along the spiral path to being part of, and as one with, the Godhead. Why a spiral path? Once again it is a question of symbolism, translating matters into terms we can understand. The tradition of the spiral or maze-type imagery is common among ancient cultures. No one can say for sure that the creators of the long barrows or chambered tombs thought in the same terms of a spiral rebirth cycle as many of us do. But it is known that the carvings which have been found in these tombs must have had some religious significance and that they were not part of an open display, because in many cases they are hidden deep within the tombs themselves.

As with many things of this nature, one must assume a good deal, never knowing the truth until the point of death. So in this light it must be assumed that prehistoric people had some sort of belief in a life or existence after death. Many of the early burial customs prove this, in the shape of grave goods. In fact, the early Celts were so convinced of this that they would issue IOUs for debts to be repaid in the next life. If one accepts that the spirit of a person survives death and lives on in an afterlife, the next step to belief in a rebirth of the same soul should not be too hard to take.

While this theory is hard to prove, at the same time there are the inexplicable things that happen to individuals. One goes somewhere and the place feels familiar, yet at the same time it is different from what you can remember of it. Even so, you know that you have never been there in this life. Or you handle a certain object and instinctively you know what it was for and how to use it. Nevertheless, you also know that there is no logical basis for your knowing about it, because the thing has been out of use for maybe 500 years or so.

Certain periods of historical time strike a sympathetic note with you. You know that, if you could be transported back to those times, you would feel at home in them. In one case, I had a vivid dream experience that I had helped to sack a temple of Isis and was cursed for it. Before anyone says, 'Oh, God, not Egypt again,' it was in London. I know where it was, yet I cannot correlate it with London as it is today.

One of the arts of the Craft is to tap into this unconscious memory and bring it back into the conscious mind. To do this one uses a form of dream-recall. Once again, it is a hard thing to explain how to go about it. One can only say that it takes an act of will to start; but when started, it is something that is hard to stop. For myself, I have found that the most productive time for this sort of activity is during that period when one is half asleep and the mind has started to wander. By fixing the mind on a certain situation that one wishes to explore, sleep comes – and with it, dreams.

The question of why one should bother to do this is often asked. Inherent in any spiritual advancement and learning is the understanding of the self. Self, that is, in the context of, 'Why have I been born the way I am? Why is my life the way it is? Why do I feel the need to look back and then go forward?' The revealing of past lives and the understanding of those lives are the only things that can throw light on present circumstances.

Without going too deeply into personal matters, I can recall something that was said to me years ago by Robert Cochrane. Three of us were sitting together talking about nothing in particular, when suddenly he looked at me and went very cold and distant. Then he said, 'John, violence and the aura of violence that surrounds you is a self-made curse of your own creating. Until you can break it, then over and over again you will pay for it.' Never were truer words spoken by any person. From what I know of my past existences, violence has always been my downfall. In the early years of this life, violence towards others was part of my life. The one lesson I should have learned by now is to reject this path or way. It has taken a long time to realize it. Next time around I might even avoid trapping myself in the same old endless circle.

By looking at past existences, you find that they hold lessons for the future. In this life, even thinking in terms of turning to the Goddess means that one no longer accepts the established faith. By turning to the Goddess, a person must accept that they have changed to the extent of realizing that their spiritual salvation is in their own hands. They must accept that the code of moral conduct they choose to live by is one of their own creation. By doing this, by symbolically cutting the Gordian knot, they take upon themselves the fate of their own salvation. No longer will they need some other person to intercede between them and the Godhead. They have advanced along the spiral path enough to be the master of their own fate. No longer is it possible for any other person to grant absolution, with just a few words, for any act committed. Each individual must be his or her judge of his or her own actions, and know and understand that, deep down, absolution cannot be granted but must be earned. The path of the Goddess was never an easy one to follow.

Though every soul is an individual, I am of the conviction that certain people are linked in some way to others as part of a group of souls in a kindred existence. Part of the spiral way is that these kindred souls advance along the path together; not as a group as such, but as a group of people who are working towards the same end. Once again, there is no way of proving that this is so. It is a matter of personal conviction. But I think that one of the factors which helped me to arrive at this conclusion was the way in which it was discussed and examined in my old coven.

Part of the conviction of this theory for me is the fact that you occasionally meet a person with whom you have an instant rapport. You instinctively know what they are thinking, and so close is this feeling of kinship that you understand them better than a brother or sister. Even though there is a vast difference in the life-styles and background of the people concerned, so that by all logical reasoning they should be totally incompatible, they are not. They feel at home in each other's company. Age, sex and upbringing, anything which logically should be the divider between them, goes by the board, because as a matter of instinctive feeling they are bound to each other and they know and feel it. These people are kindred souls.

Unfortunately, this sort of experience is not often found in a lifetime. Part of the reason for this is that each individual must find their own development within their own fate. Yet at the same time, to experience this sort of rapport with another person or group of people is a reminder that we are not alone out there in our search for spiritual development. Because of the nature of the interlinking of our kindred souls, we as individuals not only owe it to ourselves to advance spiritually; we also owe it to the others of our group.

Very often a person can be trapped into an endless circle of mistakes lifetime after lifetime. Then during one life they meet a person who has a profound influence on their thinking. It is like someone holding out a helping hand and saying, 'You've gone around and around long enough. It's about time you came on a bit and caught up with the rest of us.'

In another way, a person can be drawn into the Craft or the occult for no particular reason, even though their background and upbringing would logically indicate that they would have no interest in such subjects. When people are at this stage, very often a meeting with one person can change their whole way of thinking. Instead of being on the fringe and toying with the idea, they take the plunge and are committed to it. By this meeting, a person is no longer fixed in the one place. They have taken their first step in awareness that there is something more to life than being born, growing up, settling down to a middle-aged existence, then growing old, with death as the finish of it all. Once again, that helping hand has brought one a little further along the path towards the Goddess.

Having accepted the idea of birth, death and rebirth of the soul as a basic part of the concept of existence, the next thing to explore is the concept of magic. This is an evocative word, one that conjures up pictures ranging from the hook-nosed old witch beloved of children's books, who turns people into toads, to the horror-film satanist and black magician sacrificing a virgin to gain power from his master the Devil. Doreen Valiente, in her excellent book *Natural Magic*, has done more to explain the nature of practical magic than any author I have ever read. In this book she explains the techniques used in the magic of colours, the magic of numbers, the magic of the weather and many others. I know that there is no way in which I could possibly equal or better her work on the subject. All

I can hope to do is to present a comprehensible and generalized picture of the concept of natural magic.

Magic as such is nothing more or less than a series of natural laws. Having said this, I must qualify the statement by saying that many of these laws that we accept as natural are not the same as those understood and accepted by science today. Under the guise of research into extra-sensory perception (ESP), many of the faculties that we accept as part of our Craft are being explored and in many cases superficially explained away. Yet, underlying all this explaining-away, there is a residue of inexplicable things that no one can quite put their finger on or talk out of existence. This so-called residue is part of the magic of the faith. As a basic concept, it must first be taken on trust, explored and developed and then expanded as a practical application of inherent mental powers.

Before delving any deeper into the subject, one point must be established. There are two forms of magic. One is the magic of the self. The other form is that of supernatural effects brought about during certain rites. The first one is effected by the releasing of the inner forces of the self in a controlled manner. The other is a manifestation of an external power creating an entity, energy or force that defies logical explanation within the framework of this present existence. These are things which cannot be explained away or put down to simple chance.

In the magic of self, it is not a question of having to learn some great esoteric secret. It is rather one of rediscovering the long-dormant faculties that are part of the genetic heritage which has been handed down to us from our remote past. So just what are these faculties? Telepathy, precognition, divination, the ability to recognize and interpret omens in the form of natural phenomena, to be able to recognize and respond to instincts that have no logical foundation within rational thought.

Animals that live within the shadow of an active volcano very often show signs of fear and panic before an eruption. Birds and wild livestock very often desert the danger area. Domestic livestock show signs of tension and fear. They know in their own inarticulate and instinctive way that something threatening is going to occur. Only man voluntarily ignores all these natural omens, relying on an empiric approach and exploration before reacting, and very often getting caught out. It is then a case of disaster being 'the Will of God', ignoring the basic fact that within the human make-up is the faculty to recognize and react to natural omens. Human beings throughout their advancement in material civilization have neglected and buried these gifts deep within the unconscious self. Therefore, when an individual receives a warning of a coming danger and when that warning proves right, it is a case of 'Surprise, surprise!' all round.

To a greater or lesser extent, everybody possesses these latent powers. As with reading the Tarot cards, some people are average and not all that good, while others give a reading that goes far beyond all expectations. In my case, one reading that I had done for me gave me to understand that something I was working on would be successfully finished but that in the end I would have to let it go and expect no more from it. Not what I wanted; but in the end it happened just as it was foretold, and there was nothing I could do about it. The thing was that the person doing the reading was able to see more in the fall of the cards than just a mechanical interpretation, because she had the ability to foresee the future and had sharpened up that faculty by constant practice.

So in the search for the magic of the self, all sorts of avenues must be explored. Some people will find that they are better at one form of divination than another. In my case, try as hard as I can, I never manage to get a better-than-average score at guessing the number of letters, if any, that I shall receive the next day. Yet others of my acquaintance have the knack of being right more times than the law of averages would suggest. Once again, the predicting of mail deliveries is nothing more than a means of sharpening up a natural faculty.

One ability that I have developed is that of 'overlooking'. Some people say this should not be done; but as I have the gift, I tend to use it. By setting up a candle in a darkened room and then using it as a focal-point of concentration, I create a mental image of the place where I know the person I am 'overlooking' will be. At a certain point in time, you find you are no longer seeing a mental image but a real picture of what is actually occurring. If that person is not there, you will know, because in the case of a house or flat it will be empty. At first I found it hard to do and only saw events in a series of flashes. But practice with the co-operation of a friend enabled me to see places for longer and longer periods. Now very often when I am just sitting still, doing nothing in particular, I start picking up things concerning people I know.

Part of any individual advancement is the realization that within oneself there are submerged instincts or faculties lying dormant. Having realized and accepted this, the next stage is to bring them to the surface, explore and begin to utilize them as part of a mystic heritage that is the birthright of every individual. One point worth remembering is that these faculties should never be allowed to become the sole aim of working in themselves. They are part of you as a person. The ability to understand and use them as a stage in the opening-up and understanding of the self is the main aim in the developing of them. They create within the person the extent and limitations that can be achieved in the realizing of one's own potential.

The other form of magic is the magic of the circle. This is vastly different from the magic of the self. Not only is it different, but it resembles the legendary Sword of Damocles in nature. In the horror film portrayal we may see the archetypal black magician who in the end is destroyed by his own black arts. The same can occur with the practice of the magic of the circle. The inherent nature of circle magic is that of a potentially dangerous but neutral power, which in the case of constant misuse can and does rebound on the practitioner. The realization that there is a power or force that can be tapped, used and manipulated by a working group or a solitary magician very often leads to the assumption that, because past results have been good, the group or person concerned has some divine right to use this power in any way they see fit. Not so; every working magician is to a certain degree the servant of that power, even though on the surface they seem to be the master of it. The lesson of the exercising of any form of magical power is not that one can do it but rather one of knowing that the power is there, to be exercised with responsibility, respect and above all restraint. To think otherwise is the first step along the path of self-delusion and eventual self-destruction.

So just what is this power? In essence, magical power is nothing more or less than a physical manifestation of the Godhead, which through certain rites and rituals chooses to reveal itself to the congregation in various ways. In one form, it is a spontaneous contact at the highest level with the Goddess. On another level, it is spontaneous contact with more elemental spirits, or with the aspects of the gods and goddesses of both time and place. In another form, power may be raised within the circle to be deliberately directed and manipulated towards a certain end, usually as a force of good or evil, help or harm. This is the power in its most dangerous form, and it needs a person or group well versed in the handling, directing and earthing of this type of magic.

Probably the first physical exposure to circle magic that any newcomer to the faith will experience will be in the form of a spontaneous contact. This contact can take many aspects and relate to one individual or to the group or coven as a whole. It can take the form of an intense inner feeling, or it can express itself as a physical manifestation of a recognizable spirit form. As noted before, in a group sense the working rite is an expression of worship and devotion to the Goddess, yet on occasions the whole nature and feel of the ritual change. In all workings there is an awareness of the outside world, the feeling that, although one is in the circle, time and the outside world are still linked to the group. All of a sudden, the whole nature of the working changes. The circle closes in, giving the feeling of a definite barrier between the two worlds. In the world of the circle, time itself seems to stand still. Emotions are heightened. The sacred fire seems to burn brighter, and the light from it possesses a sharper clarity. Thoughts, ideas and emotions take on a greater depth and reality, and then there is that surge of external power.

From that moment on, the rite is in the hands of the Goddess.

As with all spontaneous contacts of this nature, everyone present will feel it within themselves. It may be a feeling of calm and peace or one of thrust and excitement. But the knowledge that something external is working on the group or coven, causing it to react in a certain way, will be felt by all present.

Within this general feeling of contact with the Goddess, one individual may receive more than the others. He or she will have been selected as the channel of the Goddess in a prophetic form. For myself, I feel that this must be treated with a certain amount of caution, as sometimes people can be overtaken by the sheer excitement of the meeting. They then start putting their own ideas into words and attributing them to the Goddess. When someone is in a trance state, it is far better for one of the officers to question them as to what they see than for the group as a whole to examine afterwards anything that was said.

As with all occult experiences, there is always the underlying doubt as to the genuineness of the occurrence. People often see what they want to see, and hear what they want to hear; so any spontaneous contact must be treated with a certain amount of caution. Very often the dividing line between illusion and truth is a very fine one. In fact, a lot of magical working is an illusion which changes into reality. One of the arts of the Craft is to recognize illusion for what it is and realize the part it plays within the magic circle.

A physical manifestation is somewhat harder to define, strangely enough. When the manifestation is seen by more than one person, you can be sure that something was there. The question then is, what and why? This question is not an easy one to answer. At one ritual at which I was present, a certain point was reached when there was a manifestation of a head. No message, just a head. It was not until much later that the persona and reason for this appearance became clear. What in fact I had seen was the God of the Winds blowing away the foundations of our group. I knew it meant something, I could feel it meant something. But it was not until future events unrolled and the group started to split up that I realized that it signified the end of our gathering.

Though this was a spontaneous manifestation of clear-cut dimensions, spelling out a certain end, there is another form of manifestation which was best summed up by an American member of the clan. She called it 'the Hidden Company'. In this case, the Hidden Company she was referring to is not so much seen as felt and partially seen: the hazy forms that seem to be part of the working but are out on the rim of the circle. This phenomenon is not something which happens immediately but something that builds up over a period of a year or so. It is as if these spirits have gradually accepted the workings of the group or coven as something linking to their past life and ways. To what extent they are attracted to the group or if the group attracts them is one of those unanswerable questions. All that can be said is that they are there and that they are a recognizable part of the coven worship and workings.

In a sense, although the destiny and direction of the coven are in the hands of the working members, there is the distinct feeling that to a certain extent the group is directed by the Hidden Company. Not in an obvious way; but there is that definite air of subtle influence being brought to bear on the members. In long-established groups, very often any new member goes through a psychic vetting. In the case of an unsuitable member, there is a definite sense of hostility and rejection of that person by the Hidden Company. To ignore this will in time lead to the weakening of the contact between the two worlds; and should disharmony continue within the group, eventually contact will be broken off. The one thing that should be stressed about this particular form of contact is that it is not a personal contact through one person. Nebulous and ill-defined though it may be, the presence of the Hidden Company is one that is felt by all and recognized by all. In this sense, the Hidden Company are perhaps the guardian spirits of the coven.

There is one form of manifestation that is widely known but very rarely practised. This is the conjuration of spirits of the lower kind, regarded by Christians as devils. While recognizing that this can be done, from a personal point of view I consider it to be a highly dangerous course to embark upon. Also, to a certain degree it is one that negates the whole reason for working.

To this extent, I suppose the aims of our old group are still valid to me. In the past, we made a conscious decision as a group to move away from the ritual workings and turn towards the mystical and devotional side of the faith. By turning to the path of conjuration, one is seeking power not for greater understanding but for the sake of power alone. Eventually this sort of power-use will lead to power-abuse and inevitable self-delusion and self-destruction. I feel strongly that there is no room for this sort of magical working within these pages. Anyone wishing to tread this path will have to find their own way.

There is one other form of spirit manifestation which has not been mentioned in this chapter. The reason for this is that it is based upon the mythos of the skull. Because of the complex relationship between history, the faith and this mythos, it is better to deal with this matter under a separate heading.

At some stage in the working career of any group, there will occur the finest experience of all – contact with the Goddess. She truly lays her finger upon you; and from that moment on, faith in her existence is transformed into certainty. At every meeting the group will call upon her to come to them and inspire them. Very rarely is this prayer answered. Often the first physical sign of her coming presence is during the dedication of the wine by the priest and priestess. When the knife is dipped into the wine in the act of symbolic sexual union, a pale blue light seems to glow from within the cup. Within that few seconds, the wine is transformed into something more than wine and is charged with the knowledge, wisdom and inspiration of her cauldron. Each person partaking of that charged cup will feel a subtle change within themselves. Though each person will feel an individual change, a common and shared knowledge that there has been change will run through the whole group.

Why this should occur at one meeting and not at

another is one of the mysteries of the faith; but occur it does. Why at any particular time is another of those unanswerable questions. Perhaps it is the make-up of the members working the rite at that particular time. Perhaps it manifests itself only to certain people within the group. As this can occur at any one of the Sabbats or Esbats, it is one of those things that you cannot pin down. All that can be said is that it can and does occur; and although it affects people in many different ways, the common theme is that everyone present has some doubt satisfied or some personal question of faith answered.

One thing that is common to all contacts of this nature is the knowing and being touched by an absolute and infinite power. Even though there may be a feeling of love and compassion flowing from the contact, there is still that aura of the cold, distant and ageless remoteness of the Goddess. For behind our concept of the Goddess and how we choose to see her, there is another power which is far more remote and which is the life force and spirit of the universe.

One aspect of the Craft which is largely overlooked today in the search for the mystic side of the faith is the art of healing and cursing. To couple them together may seem strange at first; but in effect they are opposite sides of the same coin of classical herbal lore. The witch can in effect claim descent from the healer-priestesses of ancient Egyptian and eastern cultures. As religion and medicine became more and more male-oriented and dominated until they were finally separated, the role of the healer-priestess became more and more diminished, even though her herbal lore was still as extensive. Time and the rise of the exclusively male medical profession, together with Christianity, reduced this art to the level at which the witch-healer was portrayed as the evil old crone distilling her poisons to help back up a curse. The fact that the victim sometimes died after such a cursing would most certainly have strengthened this portrayal. But behind all this lay a knowledge of both magical and herbal lore that was for centuries the only form of medical help available to ordinary people. The woman who had too many children already and just couldn't face the thought of another one would consult the old village wise woman, with her charms, spells and dose of herbal medicine. The spell worked, the woman miscarried, and the reputation of the old wise woman would be enhanced.

Today the medical role of the witch is practically non-existent; but there is another form or facet of healing – the power of absent healing – which is still an important part of the circle workings. Today there is an acceptance within the Christian Church of healing by faith, the laying-on of hands to cure the illness. Within the Craft, the concept of being able to work a rite and send out waves of healing power is an accepted practice, which works in the same way as sending out a curse. Once again, this raises the same unanswerable question: 'Why does it work?'

I for one cannot say why; but work it does, on both individual and group levels. On at least two occasions, I have worked as an individual and as part of a coven. In one case, I 'bought' a cold over the telephone, using the old Norfolk method of tying it up in a piece of string. The naughty thing is that it has to be passed on. So by one's unknotting the string and leaving it around, the first person to handle the string gets the cold.

In the instance of the coven working, I had never met the person at that time. All I knew was that we were going to do a healing. Later on, when I had got to know that person and he described his healing in his autobiography, I realized whom we had been working for and what the effect was.

Having said this, I must also say that in many cases absent healing simply does not work. There are many theories as to why a healing does or does not work, which are linked mainly to matters of faith and mental state and so on. Like everyone else who has given this a lot of thought, I have my own theory as to why this should be so.

On one plane everybody has within themselves a store of latent power or energy waiting to be tapped. With training, they should eventually be able, by looking at someone, to see within their mind a picture or colour of the afflicted area. By bringing the energy contained within themselves forward in the form of waves, they can then change the colour of the injured or affected area to a healthier and more glowing colour. In my case, I can often pick out an area of sickness, because to me it has a green aura. I see healing in the form of a warm golden light. I then visualize this light gradually diluting the green area until the green colour is non-existent. This does not mean that by this method I can cure anything and everything. I cannot, nor would I like to. To use this force or power in a prolific manner only weakens it and disperses it.

Like all these individual powers, it has first to be discovered, developed and then used sparingly. The art is not to use them any old how but to know that they are there and can be used. As with all things connected with the Craft, a price has to be paid for the using of them. One day you will find yourself trying to cure something that would be best left to orthodox medicine, and failing.

On the other plane, a coven or group healing rite is a direct plea to the Goddess to intervene in an illness. Usually this is done for a member, loved-one or friend. How this is gone about is a matter for different groups to decide upon for themselves. Some like to have a photograph of the person concerned. Others like to have something more personal, in the form of hair or nail clippings or a personal and loved object borrowed for the occasion. Other groups find that they can do just as well without anything at all, preferring to use a mental link rather than a physical one. As with all things of this nature, the timing of the working is important. Being a follower of the Goddess of the Night, I see in the lunar phases a physical manifestation of the Lady in all her aspects. In the new moon, the Lady is the Young Maid. The full moon represents the Lady as the Magna Mater. The waning moon is the phase of the Old Hag or Destroyer. The dark of the moon is the hidden side, the time of dark workings. I could no more try to work a healing during the dark of the moon than I would try a cursing at full moon. In both cases, the aspect that I would be working under would be wrong for the occasion.

In a healing, the correct time to work would be when the lunar phase is growing to the full. This is the aspect of the Goddess as the Young Maid, growing aware of her developing powers and leading towards the wisdom, compassion and understanding that are to be found in a mature, beautiful and loving Mother figure. It is to this aspect of the Goddess that we turn when looking for help, understanding and, above all, compassion.

In the circle, and while the Dance of the Mill is being trodden, everyone focuses their mind on what is being asked for. At first nothing seems to be happening at all. Then there is a subtle feeling of change in the temperature, and the feeling of being faced by a dark, soft, impenetrable barrier that all of a sudden gives way. Then wave after wave of power flows to the group, through the group and outwards from the circle. From that moment on, everyone in the circle knows that the rite has worked, that the Goddess has granted the plea. All that is then left is the feeling of being drained of energy, tired, empty and worn out. For weeks after this sort of working, there is the feeling that something has been taken away from the group. Most people feel closed down and out of contact. This is the time of rest, the time when the psychic batteries must be given a chance to recharge themselves.

Like many things of the Craft, the powers of healing are balanced by the powers of cursing. In effect, the power invoked in both cases is one and the same thing. It is only the end results that differ. Instead of transmitting the power of good through healing, the power of evil through hate is transmitted. The technique used is exactly the same; and should the Goddess grant the placing of a curse, there is still that sudden feeling of a barrier giving way and the cold, dark waves of hatred pulsing through the gathering and outwards. Once again, there is a time to do this sort of working; and once again, the time should be governed by the lunar phase. As stated above, the time of cursing is during the dark of the moon. This phase signifies the dark side of the Goddess, in the shape or form of the Old Hag or the Angel of Death. In this guise, she is the one who lines her nest with the bones of poets, the Sheela-na-Gig figure with the all-devouring sex organ. From her womb came all life – and with life came death. In this aspect she is the Goddess of Revenge.

To call on this aspect of the Goddess, any group or

coven must be certain in their own minds that there is good enough cause for this working and appeal for justice. Once this side of the Goddess is invoked and put into motion, a price will be extracted from the group. For months afterwards, the group generally feels flat and empty. The rapport and harmony that should be part of the coven or group psyche are broken, and in some cases a whole year's working can be lost. Time alone can and does heal this; but if the working has been of a particularly heavy nature, a full ritual of purification should be used, to leave behind all the negative influences generated by the cursing rite.

The rites of cursing will never appear in these pages, because they are ours and for us alone. Anyone wishing to curse will have to find their own way. The rite of purification will be given later on. Not only can this rite be used after a particularly heavy working; it can often be used to help members or friends who are down in the dumps and feel as though they are under some malign influence. The mere fact that the rite is being done for them very often gives them that lift and psychological boost which help to overcome the bad feelings they have.

I know that one of the things which will be said is that the concept of working to the lunar phases and differing aspects of the Goddess is a bit old hat, and may be considered downright primitive. I agree, it is primitive; but at the same time, these concepts have stood the test of time. Just as nature and life are a cycle of ages and seasons, so is the Goddess. In each of her faces she represents one facet of life: youth, maturity, old age, death and then the hidden time before rebirth. By working for certain ends within the framework of these aspects of her cycle, the feeling of continuity, understanding and instinctive involvement is experienced. Part of the art of the Craft is the knowing when to work, why to work at that particular time, and the reasons why that certain time-span is the right one.

One can discuss, theorize and enter into all sorts of intellectual reasonings and explanations; but there is one fact that no one can overlook or ignore, and that is that instincts and the heart speak louder and more truly than any intellectual theorizing. The concepts and workings became established in the past because they did work, and time itself has in no way invalidated the truth of them.

2 The Nature of the Rites

In the beginning there was chaos, and out of that chaos came order. With order came life, in all its many and varied forms. The culmination of this life was humanity. Human beings, thinking, feeling and evolving in what to them was a hostile environment, surrounded by the ill-understood forces of nature, to whose every whim they were a prey.

These first human beings sought for a meaning to all this in the relationship between themselves and their surroundings. Dimly at first, but with growing certainty and understanding, they realized that they were at one and in harmony with the very forces of nature which seemed hostile to them. The divinity of nature was there and was recognized; and within humanity itself a spark of that same divinity resided.

As humanity developed from the hunting existence to the more settled agricultural way of life, people became even more dependent on the forces of nature, personified as benevolent spirits. While they were still in the hunting stage, people felt that by the use of the re-enactment of a successful hunt they could, by a form of sympathetic magic, appeal to and influence the great guardian spirit of the deer, bison or whatever animal they were hunting, to send some of these animals to the hunters. Gradually, people adopted certain animals as being related to them in some way. In dark and secret places they put the bones of these animals in a ritual pattern as a thank-offering for a successful hunt. In time, groups of people began to associate more and more with a certain breed of animal. The animal in question then became increasingly associated with the guardian spirit of that group, clan or tribe. Thus one step in humanity's spiritual awareness and development was taken.

However, when a more settled life-style came about, due to their being tied to the land and the growing of crops, people found themselves ever more at the mercy of the elements. Nature in the form of the seasons had to be understood and the spirits of those seasons placated. People's very existence depended on the benevolence of nature. A bad year meant starvation, a good year life. It was little wonder that people should try to interpret and adapt the still-remembered rituals from their hunting past to meet the needs of their new circumstances.

Gradually they began to see in the seasons a mirror image of human life. As the man's seed planted within the woman grew, so the seed planted within the earth grew, matured and eventually ripened for harvesting. In the year's span from planting to harvesting, human beings could see their own lives reflected – birth, youth, maturity, old age, death and finally rebirth through the planting of new seed, as they who were once children became the parents of the next generation.

In the case of the female, she was the mysterious one, the one with the future within her. She was the child, the maiden, the mother and eventually the old barren woman who held the secrets of the tribe. As the carrier of life within herself and the deliverer of that life by giving birth, it was little wonder that people began to regard nature and the earth as a female, a Mother Goddess. Turning their eyes to the heavens, they saw the female cycle mirrored in the lunar phases. The waxing and waning of the moon were like the growing and weakening of the female fertility cycle.

Also within the phases of the moon could be seen the life cycle of humanity in general. There was the new moon, symbolic of birth and youth; the full moon, symbol of maturity and strength; the waning, the time of old age and a weakening of that strength; finally, the dark of the moon, the hidden time when no one knew where she was. Yet after the dark time, there came rebirth in the shape of the new moon. Did this symbolize the passage of the soul through life to death and then to rebirth? The evidence of grave goods being found buried with the bodies in prehistoric graves points to a belief in a separate entity or soul surviving the finality of death, and perhaps needing these goods in some way in the afterlife.

To ensure fertility in the woman, male participation was needed as well. But who would be a fitting consort for the moon, the lady of the night? Man had a symbol of himself in the sun. Like himself, at the beginning of life it held the promise of strength. By midday or mid-life, the sun was strong and at its hottest. Yet as the day progressed it grew weaker, until at sunset it was gone, leaving only the lady of the night to show her face to the waiting people.

During the year, in the seasonal changes, man saw his life mirrored. Spring was the time of youth, summer the time of maturity, winter the weakness of old age, only to be reborn in the spring again with renewed strength. Thus there were balance and harmony together, the mother, the father and the child. There was the old king, then the young king superseding the old one, only to be replaced himself by the newborn young king of the spring rebirth.

Of course, this is a simplistic approach to what in fact is a complex and many-sided aspect of humanity's growing spiritual awareness and involvement. Equally varied are the names and aspects of the Goddess and her consort and child, by whatever names they are known. Be it the rites of Adonis, the Egyptian Osiris or the European Corn Goddess myths, the sacrifice of the Divine King remains the central theme; not only remaining central to the concept but also evolving from it into the actual ritual sacrifice of a human representative of that king as a yearly tribute to the Great Mother.

Time and new thinking reduced or modified the actual ritual murder aspect of the Old Faith to where the sacrifice became the exception rather than the rule, until today the only traces of it can be found in some folk dances. For an example of this, one only has to look at 'the killing of Jack-in-the-Green' in the grounds of Hastings Castle. The dancer who plays the part of 'Jack' is dressed to represent a green bush. He dances through the town and is eventually pushed over to release the spirit of summer, or the killing of the old God-King to let the new one reign.

Times change, and with them the nature of people's

religious observances. With the passing of time, the now
formalized deities became the tutelary gods and goddesses of the new city states. As they did so, the old
simplicity and involvement within the act of worship
became lost to the congregation. Intercession with the
gods could be sought only through the medium of a
priest. The simple faith was formalized into empty ritual in
which pomp and display became the order of the day.

Finally, with the establishment of the relatively new
Christian faith as the official state religion of the Roman
Empire in the year 330, the temples of the gods were
gradually deserted or taken over. This is not to say that
Christianity as we know it became overnight the mainstay
of the empire. The Roman emperor Constantine and his
successors still maintained the fundamental maxim of
Roman law that the care of religion was the duty of the
magistrates. By the Edict of Milan in 313, in 325 at the
Council of Nicea where the Nicene Creed was ratified and
later, in 484, at the Council of Constantinople, the death
knell of the schismatic Churches within Christianity was
sounded. By imperial decree, orthodoxy was established
throughout the Roman Empire, and the sects of the
Donatists, Arians and others were declared heretical. By
this action, the foundation was laid for the future
persecutions of all those who dared to think in
unorthodox ways.

Even though paganism in all its varied forms was
defeated or, where its customs or usages were too strong,
absorbed, a powerful element of the worship of the
Mother Goddess was still carried on in the hidden places
of the Old Faith. The Mother still had her devoted
followers, even though they were isolated from each
other. The fact that the rites had to be practised in secret
meant that the more bloody aspects of the faith had to be
forgone. Instead of the sacrifice being done in the open, it
was performed in the secret glades, a token one, the
libation of drink poured in the name of the Goddess.

Because of the secrecy of the worship, the mystical side
of the Old Faith was restored. No longer was there a line
of powerful priests or priestesses controlling the rites and
interpreting the will of the gods. It was a handful of lesser

mortals practising the half-forgotten rites of their ancestors, and by doing so moving away from the established ritual to a simple involvement in the worship of the Goddess, and through her the Horned King of the woodland glades, *Rex Nemorensis*.

Later persecutions damaged the old ways even more. Belittled and abused, the Old Faith appeared to degenerate into nothing more than small groups, usually of old, spiteful women casting malign spells on neighbours' cattle or stopping horses until a toll had been paid, and so on. But hidden within the cycle of nature was the Goddess. Forbid her worship, deny her the congregation, yet she will still be there, for her spirit is the very spirit of the land itself. Battered, fragmented, yet never quite finished, the knowledge of the Lady still lingers on. Her rites are still observed; not only observed, but with a growing number of worshippers.

To many, the orthodox faiths have lost their fire, have become enmeshed in liturgy and are failing to meet the needs of the age. Just as the Roman Catholic Church by its own actions gave birth to the Protestant movement, which in turn, when established, led to the appearance of the Nonconformist movements, so the worship of the Goddess and all that is involved by following her cult is attracting new followers. Slowly more and more people are hearing her call, because to some she is an alternative to today's orthodox faiths.

To follow her ways is to attune oneself to the rhythm of nature, to tap into and try to understand the forces within oneself as well as being able to respond to the external forces that are part of the mystic cosmos; to rediscover the almost lost senses that were the Old Gods' gifts to humanity. The power to be able to look into the future in all its forms; the ability to foresee the results of any word, deed or action and to prophesy the outcome. To be able to reach back into the past and see our present time as part of that past; to be able to recognize and know that existence is like a spiral, and that it will take many lifetimes to travel in and at last to find the truth behind the many faiths.

By following the ways of the Lady, her consort and the young Horned King, we are turning to something that is

instinctively part of our heritage. As it is part of the cycle
of life itself, we must be part of that cycle as well. From the
moment of birth to the moment of death, we are involved
in that cycle.

Part of the magic of the Old Faith is the knowing and
accepting of this. To accept life, in some cases to be an
instrument of destiny within that life; sometimes to try to
change the rhythm of that life in some small way. For to
change life, one must change oneself also, which in turn
can lead to greater understanding and involvement. Only
by seeking, understanding and involvement will the Old
Faith yield up its secrets of inspiration, understanding and
evolvement within oneself and one's chosen group. By
giving, one receives, and the balance is maintained.

History and Myth

Having read this far, by now the reader must be thinking,
'Hold on – this isn't witchcraft as I know it!' In this, they
are correct. These rites do not follow the generally
accepted picture of witchcraft. Yet, at the same time, the
inspiration that went into the creating of these rites
reaches back to a tradition far older than the one generally
written about. From time immemorial, there has been a
faith or cult devoted to the concept of the Goddess. Call
her Diana, the Magna Mater, the Corn Goddess or the
Great Earth Mother, to many cultures she was the living
Goddess and was worshipped as such. Time itself, plus
the gradual male dominance of religion, unseated the
priestess from her pre-eminence. Conquest and subju-
gation of tribal groups brought about change and
modification of the concept. The gods of a beaten people
became the population of the underworld to the
conquerors. The living faith changed to suit the times and
situations.

Today people look towards the Celtic pagan faiths or
beliefs as a source of inspirational tradition, in much the
same way as others have looked to the East for their
inspiration; in some ways rightly so, mainly on the
grounds that the Celtic myths have been examined,
explored and written about. In fact, they represent the

main root-source of modern British paganism. Yet, as they stand, they are not English witchcraft. The true English witchcraft spanned the gap between the old Anglo-Saxons and the general acceptance of Christianity by the population as a whole.

This is the faith that was lost. Belittled and scorned by the Church, preached against and its god turned into a devil. This is the knowledge that was shattered; and with it, part of the spirit of both race and land. For in the spirit of the land were the rhythms of the English roots.

What is known of the faith was written by its enemies; and, through a long catalogue of pain and suffering meted out to those who dared to think differently, there are glimpses of the faith they died for. Unfortunately, there is not enough to form a sound basis to build upon. Instead, whether as a group or as individuals, each of us must find our own way or path to the portals of the castle. What is written in the following pages is our way of doing so. It works for us, and what more can you ask than that?

One of my favourite myths concerning the origins of the Craft is the story of Aradia, the daughter of Diana, fathered upon the Goddess by her brother Lucifer. Diana, seeing the suffering of the poor and weak, instructed Aradia in the arts of the Craft and then sent her to earth to form and instruct the secret gatherings of witches. This Aradia did; and among the secrets she passed on to her followers were the secrets of poisons, the raising of storms (a charge which was to figure prominently in later witch trials) and how to curse those who refused to help their fellow men and women.

When the time came for Aradia to rejoin her mother, one of the instructions she left behind was that the followers of witchcraft should gather at the full of the moon to pay homage to Diana, with feasting, dancing and music, hailing her as the Queen of the Heavens. In exchange for this worship, Diana would gradually instruct them in the unknown arts of magic. Of course, this is only the bare bones of the story, as given by Charles Godfrey Leland in his book *Aradia: or the Gospel of the Witches*, first published in 1899. However, enough has been mentioned to establish a connection between Diana as the lunar

goddess of witchcraft and the witch faith; also to establish
the sacred dance, music and the feast as part of the rites,
and, above all, the reason why some witches consider
themselves to be part of 'Diana's darling crew, who pluck
your fingers fine'. (see p.162)

In reality, behind the rather light-hearted myth of the
origins of the Craft, there is a darker side of the Goddess.
What her name would have been in some other and less
literate cultures, we will never know. The Greeks knew
her as the goddess Hecate, and from their description of
her, she is recognizable to us today. Ancient Hecate, older
than the Olympian gods themselves, with her triple
powers extending to the heavens, the earth and the
underworld. With her three aspects reflected in the phases
of the moon, she is the Young Maid, the Mature Mother
and finally the Old Hag in the form of the Pale-Faced
Goddess. A place where three ways meet is sacred to her
as the Triple Goddess.

Within the faith, and certainly one of its most basic
tenets, is the cult of the Horned God, or the Dying God in
the shape of the sacrifice of the Divine King. It was this
living representative on earth of the God that became 'the
Devil', since, by accepting kingship, he had accepted the
fate that was the lot of the Divine King and Incarnate God,
namely that of a sacrificial death.

As the faith became more broadly based and organized,
on an extended tribal/mini-state basis, the idea of the
divine substitute became established – the mock king
paying the price for the true king. In this way the cult
gradually evolved into a more recognizable state
pantheon, such as was found in Greece and Rome. At the
same time, the division between the gods and man
became more pronounced. The price once paid with
human blood on the altars of the gods was now paid with
animal blood, a substitute life for the human one. Even
then there was the recognition that in some ways a king
was set apart from the rest of humanity and reigned only
by the grace of the gods as a servant of the gods. Only
when called to power through the blood royal, the tokens
of office given to him by a priesthood, could a man
become the king, and to raise a hand against him became

sacrilege. To strike the gods' anointed one was to strike at the gods themselves. Thus a long line of priest-kings would come into its own.

It must be realized that Christianity, when it became the recognized faith of the western world, was nothing more than a very thin veneer overlaying a predominantly pagan population. In many cases, a kingdom was Christian only for the lifetime of a particular ruler. Many of the so-called Christian kings in fact held dual allegiance, with altars to both the Christian God and the pagan gods. At the same time, the bulk of the population would still carry on the customs and faith of their ancestors. There was very little the Church could do about it. The organized Western Church at that time simply was not strong enough. Not only that, but Rome had to deal with the schisms within its own ranks first.

Rather than the fanciful picture of a pious peasantry as painted by the Church chroniclers of the time, the reality was that of a peasantry gathering at night with the old priesthood of thirteen, to worship the Horned God and, through him, the Goddess. The priesthood or covens of priests and priestesses in any given district would have been led by the Incarnate God, the horn-wearing living representative of that Horned God. Each coven in that given district would have been led by their own representative of the god. In the forms of the Magister of the coven, and helped by the Maid of the coven, he would lead the group in the rites of worship. This was the 'Devil' that the Church would later have to deal with.

It was not until the hereditary ruling classes became firmly committed to the new Church that Christianity was able to start the long-drawn-out battle against European paganism. Until then, the Church had to compromise and settle for an outward conformity. In fact, there is some evidence to suggest that a few of the Anglo-Norman kings were Christian in name only and that other notable historical figures could also be suspected of being members of the Old Religion. For instance, King William Rufus, Joan of Arc, Gilles de Rais, the Fair Maid of Kent and Edward III, just to name a few mentioned in the books of Dr Margaret Murray, *The Witch Cult in Western Europe, The God of the Witches* and

The Divine King in England. If the evidence is correct, this shows just how high into society the old faith must have reached.

In the first of the witch trials,* it was only the humbler members of the faith who were brought to trial, and it is from these records, biased though they are, that a picture of the organization of the faith can be built up. In the first instance, a few villages would each have its local witch, male or female, and it was these who could make up the coven for a small area. These covens in their turn would be part of a greater gathering of a district. Over all these interconnected covens would be the Incarnate God on earth, the Grand Master. It was in his name that the whole gathering would be summoned for the Sabbats, and for these the leaders of the individual covens would act as officers for the meeting. It also meant that the Grand Master, in his position as the Incarnate God and through the network of covens, had his finger on the pulse of his area. He knew what was going on, who was doing what and selling what, and where to find a willing buyer. He could then use the old ploy of, 'Go to a certain place and there you will meet a short dark man who will offer you such and such' for whatever it was that was being sold. Also, he would be in the position to know who was being laggard in paying due respect to the Master and the priesthood, and very soon that person would find their crops damaged overnight, and so on. In short, until the system was broken up, the countryside was largely under the sway of the followers of the Old Religion.

In looking at the witch trials, and ignoring the ecclesiastical elaborations in the evidence, it is possible to re-create some of the rituals and feelings that were held by members of the faith. Also from these trials, it can be seen how the following of the Old Religion became more and more isolated, fragmented and eventually reduced to a

---

* Early records are naturally scanty, and it would be impossible to say with certainty what was the date of the first witch trial. However, according to Montague Summers in his *Geography of Witchcraft*, the earliest recorded witch trial in England took place in 1209. This is confirmed by C.L'Estrange Ewen in *Witch Hunting and Witch Trials* and its sequel *Witchcraft and Demonianism*.

handful of covens or groups practising half-forgotten rites, and because they had to be inward-looking, keepers of fragmentary bits of the knowledge that was once the wisdom of the old faith.

In spite of what the Church said, these people were not 'devil-worshippers', as made out at the trials. Their God was far older than the Christian God. Nor was the Old Religion in any way oppressive, unlike the Church with its tolls and tithes. In fact, what does shine through from the trial records is that witches enjoyed being members of their faith and looked forward to the meetings.

In a practical sense, the witch, having knowledge of herbal medicine, would be the village healer. In a spiritual way, the witch was the only force available to deal with localized crime. The magical powers held by witches gave them the ability to 'smell out' wrongdoing, in much the same way as the African witchdoctor does. On another level, they were able to deal with ghosts, demons and the evil spirits that haunted the minds of early men and women. In times of trouble, it was the witch who was turned to, because the witch priesthood had the power and the knowledge to deal with things. People became witches because they wanted to, rather than conforming to a religion out of fear.

One thing that is noticeable from the trial records is that membership of the faith was something that was handed down through the family. Another is that most of the witches brought to trial were female. The reason for this is simply that in the days when the magician-prophet was an honoured and accepted member of any royal Court, as in the case of Merlin, the male witch tended to be the adviser on the more important aspects of Court life, especially politics. The female witch dealt with the more homely and domestic things. She was more or less the healer-priestess of the hearth and home. Christianity eventually meant that the old magician-prophet lost his position in the royal Court, being replaced as adviser by high-ranking clerics. The female witch as a priestess-healer to the ordinary person took a lot longer to root out and destroy.

One of the reasons for this intense hatred of the female witch was her claim to be a priestess. In the time when the

Church regarded woman as unimportant and a mere chattel of her husband (only a male priest would call the pains of childbirth 'kindly'), for a woman to claim the title of priestess struck at the very roots of orthodox society.

Another reason to be considered is that women are often the most faithful followers of any religion. When men leave the churches and temples half empty, it is women who still carry on the worship. Hence, while the male witch lost his position as Court adviser-cum-astrologer, the woman still fulfilled her role as priestess of the Old Gods. In a way, it is through women and their devotion to the faith that it survived the persecutions, battered and fragmented though it is. It was the devotion of women to the Goddess and to the incarnate figure of the Horned God that has carried the knowledge down through the years. It is also the reason why in our rites we have given a place of honour to the woman as the Lady and priestess of the coven.

In the same train of thought, yet still within the basic philosophy of the faith, we have re-aligned our thinking concerning the role of the Incarnate Horned God–leader of the coven. Historically, the leader of the coven was always considered to be the living representative of the Sacrificial Divine God-King. Within this person there was the manifested essence of the Godhead, the spirit of the God in living form on earth. Sacrificed in his prime, the spirit of the God would then transfer itself to the body of the Young Horned King. In this way, the incarnate spirit of the God was kept strong. An old and weakened king was in effect an old and weakened god.

As the concept of the cult changed, the actual sacrifice of the king was replaced with the appointing of the willing Divine Substitute, the Mock King. This concept of the substitute ruler was still manifesting itself in classical times through the festival of the Lord of Misrule, the Saturnalia, with the slaves becoming the mock kings and their owners the servants. Sir James Frazer has given us a detailed description of this, and many other matters connected with the sacrifice of the Divine King, in his famous work *The Golden Bough*. There is still a trace of this concept in the Church, with the celebration of the custom of having a 'Boy Bishop' for a day.

Later, the idea of the substitute human sacrifice was modified to that of an animal sacrifice, usually the living representative of the totem spirit of the group. In the sense that the Magister of any coven is the direct descendant of the sacrificial living God, it can be understood how the seven-year cycle of office with the substitute animal sacrifice at the end of it came about. Also, and to a greater degree, how the office of Magister has lost its Divine King overtones and has now come to mean the priest-leader of the coven. In a sense, he is still the 'Devil', but the god-like attributes have reverted back to the mystical spirit-form of the Old God and his mother-consort, the Goddess.

No longer is the Magister the Incarnate God of the coven. To us, the Horned God is represented by the coven stang, the horned ash staff which stands outside the portal or gateway of the circle. Thus invoked, he is the guardian spirit of the entrance to the realm of the circle. He is the spirit of the countryside, in the guise of the Oak King and the Greenwood Lord, the reincarnated spirit of the Old God reborn within the body of the new one at the May Eve rites. He is also the old leader of the Wild Hunt, Herne with his hounds, carrying off the souls of the dead into the underworld. All these ideas are bound up in the symbology of the stang, insofar as the stang becomes the icon of the God.

With the placing of the priestess once again at the head of the rites, many of the duties that once belonged to the Magister are now hers. Where once the Magister and the Maid would have charged the cup, it is now the Lady and the Officer of the East who do it. In the past, the masked, horned figure, with a candle set between the horns, would have presided over the rite and the feast afterwards. Now the stang serves the same purpose. With a lighted candle between the prongs of the pitchfork head, and the animal mask below them, the stang recalls the memory of the Horned God and the Totem Spirit who was the sacrificed guardian of the coven.

In the same way, the crossed arrows mounted on the shaft of the stang recall the old magical workings of the rituals for good hunting. There is one aspect of the Goddess that is very often overlooked, and that is Diana the Goddess of the Hunt. It was to that aspect of her that the horned, masked figure of old would dance his sacred dance and make his ritual offerings, in the days when the people depended on hunting for their food. (Incidentally, a pair of crossed arrows is the symbol of the pre-dynastic Egyptian goddess Neith.)

By transferring the now symbolic attributes of the Incarnate God-leader of the coven to the coven stang, in effect the human who was once recognized as the living God on earth no longer has to pay the old demanded blood price, with either his own blood or that of a substitute. In this sense, even though the rites have moved away from the primitive workings, the concept of who and what the Horned God stood for has not altered. By invoking him in the spiritual sense, rather than by worshipping the living representative, it means that the more authoritative form of coven leadership is done away with. No longer should any one person be able to say, 'I am the Master. What you learn, you learn from me, as I choose to show you.' Instead, with our way of working, there is no great secret to be passed on. There are only our rites of worship, and these are open to all who wish to follow our ways.

Each and every one of us must seek to develop their own self; to discover within themselves what they want to gain from the faith; and, above all, to realize that within the faith they are perhaps looking for an answer to certain unfulfilled longings. To what extent the faith serves to ful- fil these longings is up to the individual. Only by joining in the worship of the Goddess can a person get a glimpse of what it all means. To stand on a hilltop on a moonlight night, opening yourself up to the Goddess – only then can you get the feel of the forces around you, the aura of the powers that seem part of the very air itself.

In time, and with the correct frame of mind, you can and will become as one with this power for a short while, and in that joining there is the feeling of linking up with the past. In that linking comes understanding, and with that understanding the realization that this is something you have experienced before. In this way, the echoes from the past become linked to the realities of today, and both in turn lead to a growing awareness of the future lives that will have to be lived in the lifetimes to come. Above all, in that growing awareness is the express belief that each of these lives should bring us closer and closer to the realization of some of the awesome and eternal splendour of the creation and re-creation of life and nature that is to be found in the concept of the Godhead. Only by understanding of self – and, if need be, the changing of self – can there be the opening-up and blossoming of the individual soul under the influence of the external power that is the inspirational wisdom of the Goddess.

One of the great disappointments concerning the history of the Old Faith is the lack of written records. By this, I mean records written by members rather than by the opposing forces of orthodox Christianity. Yet because the Old Religion was the religion of nature and the countryside, a lot of old country lore and fireside tales contain within them fragments of what was once a large body of matter pertaining to the craft. Accelerating changes in life-style, from the rural to the urban, mean that this lore is being lost faster than ever; and with this loss, there is the loss of some of the understanding, logic and knowledge that are the inheritance of the craft. What is left can be worked on; but in most cases any conclusions arrived at must be treated as supposition or probability, in the light of existing evidence. It is a matter of re-examining certain events and persons in the light of your own knowledge of the Old Faith.

To illustrate this point, one only has to look at the story of King Richard II and the Peasant's Revolt of 1381. The young King met the common people and their leaders at Smithfield, where, according to contemporary reports, the rebel leader Wat Tyler came to the King 'in a haughty fashion'. The upshot of this meeting was that Tyler was mortally wounded. The King rode across the green towards the mob, crying, 'Sirs, will you shoot your King? I am your captain, I will be your leader. Let him who loves me, follow me!' Instead of a flight of arrows and a slaughtered royal party, Richard turned his horse and led the rebels into open country. A hastily gathered relieving force later found the King in the Clerkenwell fields, still sitting on his horse, surrounded by the leaderless rebels and arguing with them.

At this point there are questions raised that have to a certain degree been answered, though not all that convincingly, in an orthodox way. Only days before, this same mob had had the most powerful and richest lords and clerics in the land cowering behind strong walls in fear of them. In the first meeting between the King and the insurgents at Mile End, in spite of royal promises of reform, the mob was still posing a threat to the established order. Yet a few days later this same young King, with just a few words, took over a now uncontrolled and leaderless army of rebels. How? Knowingly or unknowingly, the young King Richard had by his words 'I will be your leader' placed himself in the position of the Divine King, head of the Old Religion. Even if Richard, brought up as he was to see himself as a Christian prince, may not have known the heritage he was claiming with his words, there were many amongst the crowd with enough knowledge of the Old Faith to realize that in the eyes of that faith he was now the God on earth, and that by killing the King they would be killing that living God.

To accept this means accepting the fact that England was not the Christian country that history would have us believe. There are few scholarly works on the witch trials of Britain, and in most standard history books witch trials and the Old Religion receive no mention at all. All we get is a picture of a pious peasantry which in 1381 rose against their masters, burned manors and priories and executed Simon of Sudbury who was both the Primate and the chancellor of England, and also the Lord Chief Justice – hardly the actions of a God-fearing Christian people.

In the person of Richard Plantagenet, they had the descendant of a line of kings whose family were reputed to have claimed, 'From the Devil we came and to the Devil we go.' Looked at again in the light of the 'Devil's' being the God of the Old Religion, what was being said in reality was, 'From a long line of Divine Kings we came, and to the Old God whose representatives we are, we return in death.' By saying, 'I will be your leader,' Richard took upon himself the mantle of his ancestors, the divine Plantagenet kings.

Instead of reading official or accepted history as a single

subject, then reading the history of the witch trials as another subject, both must be read as complementary to each other, because they are two different sides of the same coin. Only by combining the two can what is left of the matter or lore of England be rediscovered.

In the same train of thought, there are many other things worth looking at again. Among these are definitely the tales of Robin Hood. On the surface, they are a collection of straightforward stories concerning an outlaw who lived in a forest and led a band of jolly fellow-outlaws. Superb archers to a man, they used their prowess with the longbow to rob the rich and help the poor. The outlawed leader of the band had at some time suffered an injustice which had stripped him of his rightful place in society. Outlaw though he was, his loyalty and that of his men was to the king. In most stories the king in question was reputed to be Richard the Lionheart.

One thing that must be recognized is that the ballads of Robin Hood as we know them were first written down some time in the fourteenth century, though stemming from a long oral tradition. It should also be noticed that attached to the mainstream of this tradition are various historical persons. In this sense, Robin Hood and his band of men became not so much a living group of people, as an ideal, a hope or, if you like, an earthly saviour and defender of the common people.

Throughout history, there have been many attempts to give a name to the man behind the legend: Eustace de Foville, Fulk Fitzwarin, Adam Bell and, strangely enough, one Robin Hood who was known to have held land in Wakefield, to name but a few. Another view is that Robin Hood is derived from Hodskin, the old Anglo-Saxon wood sprite who later became Robin Goodfellow. It should come as no surprise to find that the same Robin Goodfellow is none other than the Green Man or the spirit of spring found in many old morris dances. The Green Man whose effigy was carved by masons on a boss in the cloisters of Norwich Cathedral, in the transept of Llantilio Crossenny church in Monmouthshire, among the decorations of Rosslyn Chapel near Edinburgh and in many other sacred edifices. The Green Man whose smiling face appears among the carvings on the front of one of the oldest inns in Sussex, at Alfriston. The same Robin whom the General Assembly of the Church of Scotland petitioned King James VI in 1577 and again in 1578 to ban, in connection with the performing of plays featuring Robin Hood, King of the May, on the Sabbath day, mainly because of the unseemly ribaldry of the vulgar people on these occasions.

This was a recognition by an established Church that there was more to these tales than just a straightforward story, fictional or otherwise; more to Robin Hood than just a band of outlaws living a merry life in Sherwood Forest. One generally accepted theory regarding the story is that the common people saw Robin as the law-defying, anti-establishment hero, recognizing in him a natural champion of those who had suffered injustice at the hands of both State and Church.

At the same time, in these stories no blame is laid on the king for these injustices, only on the royal officials. In fact, the one strong theme running through the whole of the saga is the individual loyalty to the king shown by the common people. This was in a time when (unlike today when government and throne are separate institutions) the king and the state were more or less one and the same thing. Yet at no time is any blame for the corruption of the royal officials laid at the feet of the King who appointed them. Also noticeable is the devotion shown to Holy Mother Church, with special reverence being shown to the Virgin. Yet at the same time it was the wealth of Holy Mother Church that was being heisted by Robin, and it was the spiritual leaders of that same Church who were being held hostage, ridiculed and held to ransom. Moreover, we are asked to accept that these people could see Holy Mother Church as an abstract concept separate from the activities of its leaders, without realizing that by robbing the Church the outlaws were in fact robbing St Peter of some of his pence. As the saying goes, 'If you will believe that, you will believe anything.'

Just supposing Robin and his band of merry men are re-examined in the light of the Old Religion, what then? Firstly, you have a full coven, including the Maid in the shape of Marian, the only woman who receives any mention by name as a member of the band in the ballads.

In spite of her living in the forest with a gang of healthy, virile males, there is no record or tradition of any sexual relationship. Far from it; in fact, Marian was placed on a pedestal and treated more as the Queen of the Greenwoods than anything else.

In the battle for the hearts and minds of the ordinary people, Robin comes out of it as hands down the clear winner. People living in grinding poverty could have grown rich by turning him in; but they didn't. Part of the loot taken by the band was reputed to have been passed on to the needy. Perhaps in Robin there was a personification of the commoners' resentment of the ruling classes; resentment against a system that was alien to them, a system in which the faith of their ancestors had become 'the cult of the Devil'. Instead of being able to share in the rituals of their faith with understanding and knowledge, they had to attend a church in which the articles and mysteries of faith had to be preached to them, usually by someone little better in status than they.

Perhaps at some time there *was* a Robin Hood – or, considering the number of place-names connected with him, a number of Robin Hoods. But instead of being outlaws in the conventional sense, they were outlaws because they were the priestly followers of the Old Religion and the Old God. Then it became understandable why they were sheltered, aided and even a hidden part of the peasant's life. For it would be to them that he would turn to placate the evil spirits and demons that haunted the minds of medieval people. When he or his animals fell sick, the herbal remedies needed to heal them were part of the old witch lore and knowledge. It was either the old wise man or woman to whom he would have to go. At that time, Mother Church, mainly through the monastic orders, certainly had a knowledge of herbal medicine; but how far down the class lines it would have extended no one really knows. In most cases, I suspect, not very far. It would be to the old wise man or woman whom the peasant would turn for his healing and that of his family. So more especially would his wife, when she was having a baby. Can we imagine celibate monks and nuns being very good at midwifery? But there was an old saying: 'The better the midwife, the better the witch.'

Sometimes hard cash would be needed, to pay off the hated heriot and other tallages. Only by going to the Lord of the Greenwoods could the peasant get the money – that self-same cash taken from the Church or from wealthy traders. Who can blame him when, instead of looking to the Christian God in heaven for help, except in a token conformity, he turned to his old God on earth, the horned, masked figure of the coven leader?

Little wonder that the peasant, wrapped up in his knowledge of his God in a recognizably human form, saw in Robin the God that was human. Outlawed and forced into the greenwoods, the living representative of that God and the priesthood were still there, to serve the congregation as they always had. To the knowing, singing the ballads of Robin Hood was not just singing songs about an outlaw and his merry men cocking a snook at the establishment. It was an expression of belief in the old ways, a way of passing on a memory of the old ways; and in others, like the slave who spat in the master's food before serving it, a secret act of defiance, something to be kept hidden from *them*.

Even though the stories, when written down, gradually lost their meaning over a long period of time, there was and still is an element of magic in them. Through books and later films and television, the story of Robin Hood lives on. Indeed, it not only lives on but has spread through a far wider audience; for wherever the Anglo-Saxon race went, the story of Robin Hood went with them. Hidden in that story and travelling with it, are still to be found the few remaining hints of the ideals of the Old Religion. Even in the death of Robin there are echoes of the mourning for the sacrificed Divine King. Only this time, instead of awaiting the joyful spring rebirth of the new Young King, only the stories remain, and hidden within them are the memories of the old priesthood of the beloved Old Religion.

There are endless stories from the past that can be re-examined with knowledge of the Old Religion as a new way of seeing them. The one thing, of course, is that this is purely speculative and should be treated in the light of 'possibly', 'could be' or 'maybe'. But what this sort of research does indicate is that the faith now called the Old Religion *is* old, not just something thought up by a handful of cranks. Though the Goddess is known by as many names as there were different cultures, the basic concept of her worship – and, through her, that of the Horned God and the Young Horned God-King – was a universal concept enshrined within the death and resurrection cycle of both humanity and nature.

Also, and perhaps the most important point, the faith was a fluid and dynamic one, able to absorb changes of emphasis on certain aspects of it while remaining true to the basic theme. One has only to look at the way in which the theme of the Horned Sacrificial God came to be the Incarnate God on Earth to later covens. Yet, at the same time, behind him was another figure, half hidden, half forgotten perhaps; but she was still the Goddess, queen of both night and the heavens, and worship was still paid to her through the Horned God-King of the coven or clan.

In a modern sense, the aims, aspirations and reasons for worshipping the Goddess have changed. In the past, many of the followers were members because to them it was a familiar part of their lives and was as natural to them as eating, drinking and breathing. Without a doubt, most of us are conservative in nature – that is, conservative in a non-political sense. Even today, many people who are not regular church-goers in the accepted sense still marry in church, with all the trimmings, including the white wedding-dress, even though they may have been living together for years before the ceremony. In the same way, they have their children baptized, as something that is 'done'. In short, they are 'wheeled Christians' – pushed to church in the pram, driven in the bridal car and then carried to church in the hearse. It was this inbuilt conservatism in the past that would have made people turn to the familiar rather than to the new-fangled Christian Church.

At the same time, there were those who joined and remained members of the Old Religion through choice, in spite of all the laws to the contrary and the appalling danger they placed themselves in by doing so. They remained staunch and true to their gods and their faith.

Even in the face of a rising tide of zealous Christian persecution, they and their children remained true, as the witch trials prove; and now that being a practising witch is no longer a matter of law-breaking in a civil sense, those who call themselves witches have picked up their mantle.

However, when picking up this mantle we must remember that we are not the same people as they were. Our aims and ideas are different. What we look for in the faith and what we hope to gain from the faith are different from their aspirations. Unlike them, we have no helping hand to take us through an age-old and hallowed initiation. Instead, we have to find our own way and build on the work of others. No longer do we look for the same things in the faith as they did. Times change and so do aspirations; and in this sense we are not bound by a long and traditional form of worship or thinking. Instead, we are free to build our own castles; free to create our own concepts and understanding.

In most cases, we know what we look for in the faith; and though differing from the hopes and aspirations of past witches and followers, we still subscribe to the same broad concept of the Goddess, the Old Gods and the rites as they did. Like them, we look to the Goddess for our inspiration and spiritual understanding. To what extent we find this is more or less up to ourselves. We can work at one level, not advancing from there, with total satisfaction; or we can look to the rites to give us that little extra that crosses the borderline between merely working and inspirational working; the knowledge that behind what is being worked on one plane is another plane – and, beyond that, still another.

Perhaps it is the quest for what lies beyond this plane that is the inspiration which drives people to look beyond the workings of this world and urges them to explore the sacred drama, the wordless rite and spell that are the magic of illusion. It is in these first steps beyond the basic rites that another corner of the veil is lifted, and the illusion becomes reality itself.

II The Coven

1 The Coven

Before setting out the rituals for the Great Sabbats in detail, it seems necessary to explain the structure of the coven and how it works. The full coven membership should be fixed at thirteen people. Where possible, the congregation should consist of six men and six women. The thirteenth person should be female, and she will stand apart from the rest of the coven. She is known as 'the Lady'.

Under her direction will be four officers, known as North, South, East and West. North and South are always female. North should be the older of the two, and the colour of her robe should be black. South, being the younger, should wear brightly coloured clothing in the circle. East and West are always male, and while East wears bright robes, West tends to wear darker clothing, and his cloak is always hooded.

The Lady

The Lady holds her office by selection and occupies it for as long as she feels able and willing to do so; but she must renew her oath of office every seven years. Her duties start off by dedicating the circle, then leading everyone into the circle by assisting them to step over the broomstick or besom which is laid to mark the point of entry. (Just what this besom signifies and how it is placed will be explained in the appropriate section later.) With the help of East, she dedicates the cakes and wine and closes the ritual at the end. Her place in the circle is to the north, and she is the observer, the bridge or link and the channel through which the power flows.

The other duty of the Lady is oath-taking. The oath of initiation into the coven is taken in her presence. The oath of full membership after a year and a day's service is administered by her, and all four officers take their pledge of office under her direction. She also presides over the settling of disputes; and should the cause arise, she will pronounce the sentence of banishment on any member. She presides over all coven activities, and in the circle her word is law.

North

The Lady of the North is the Dark One, the Hag. She represents the dark side of the Goddess, the Pale-Faced One who presides over the cauldron. At the Hallowe'en ritual, her domain is in the second circle. It is she who with West dedicates the apples and the cider. Cold and dark is her aspect, and dark are her thoughts. Strong, silent and powerful should be her character, and wisdom should be her trademark.

South

The Lady of the South represents the younger aspect of the Goddess. She is the mature one, kindly and warm, the loving mother. She is the one who recalls what has transpired at the Candlemas ritual. It is she who calls in the Lady for the cutting of the cornstalk. Warm and gentle is her nature, for she represents the Mother-aspect of the Goddess. Kindness and benevolence are her trademarks.

East

He is the young one, and the bright morning light is his aspect. In the circle he is the man who serves the Lady at the dedication of the cakes and wine. He is the keeper of records. It is he who brings the initiate into the circle. Bright and lively should be his aspect, in harmony and balance with the Lady of the South. He is the one who raises any group matters at the meetings, and records all the decisions taken. His trademarks are those of life and fire.

West

He is the male balance to the Lady of the North. He is the Lord of the Mound, and his aspect is that of the old Celtic God, Gwynn ap Nudd. At Hallowe'en he serves the Lady of the North in her circle. He also is the one who gives the coven light as they cross from one circle to the other. Sombre is his clothing, and sombre is his aspect, for he is the guardian of the mound and the gates of the underworld. The Hounds of Hell are his to control, and under the name of Herne he leads them out on the Wild Hunt at Candlemas. He is the holder of hidden wisdom, and strength and silence are his trademarks.

The Membership

From the foregoing it will be seen that the running of the coven is vested in the four officers and the Lady. The rest of the group will usually be comprised of two sorts of members, namely those who are fully initiated and new members still serving the year-and-a-day's apprenticeship. In the case of full members, they should be capable, willing and experienced enough to take over any of the offices which are appropriate to their sex. In the case of illness of any of the officers, the Lady will call on any full member to fill that office in a temporary capacity. If the Lady is unable to officiate, it is the duty of East to select her replacement from one of the female officers or members, provided of course that the Lady has not delegated her duties beforehand.

In the event of the Lady or any of the officers being unable or unwilling to renew the seven-year oath of office, names will be put forward to be voted on by all full members. In the case of the Lady's standing down, the oath of acceptance will be administered by the longest-serving officer.

At any time a full member can claim the right to set up their own group or coven within the tradition. Any member wishing to do so should be encouraged and assisted by all members of the main coven. The only condition to this aid is that the member concerned must take a pledge in front of the full coven, to hold firm to the aims, ideas and workings of what now becomes the clan. They must also acknowledge the suzerainty of the Lady over the newly formed coven.

In exchange for this pledge, he or she is entitled to claim a full copy of all rituals. They may also call on other members to rank as temporary officers until the group is strong enough to select its own officers. They may call on the Lady of the main coven to arbitrate in any dispute that cannot be settled within the new coven. They are also able to bring any or all of the members of the new coven to the main coven meetings, knowing that, as members of the clan, there is a place saved for them within the circle; because from the one seed planted come the many.

The Initiate

Initiates must be vouched for by one or more members who have personal knowledge of them. It is the duty of the full member sponsoring them to explain just what they are letting themselves in for. The next stage is to introduce them to the full coven at one of the minor meetings. This gives the initiate and the coven a chance to look each other over in none-too-serious circumstances.

If the initiate feels hesitant at this stage, they are in no way to be influenced by any member of the coven. To join or not to join is a matter of free will and not of any undue influence by others. If he or she decides that they wish to continue with the coven, it is the duty of the sponsor to explain the commitment more fully to that person. The next step is for the initiate to be brought to the Officer of the East in an informal way. East will then make sure that they really do understand what is being asked of them.

First, that they will take an oath at the next meeting to serve a year and a day's apprenticeship.

Second, that they will never reveal to anyone the workings within the rites that are done, irrespective of the aims and objectives involved in those workings.

Third, as all members take on a coven name at their initiation, the true name of any member must never be revealed to an outsider.

Fourth, that they will hold true to the faith, the clan and the coven in all things.

Fifth, that they will accept and abide by all judgments pronounced on them by the Lady in the presence of the coven.

Sometimes, after a few months, the initiate may feel that they no longer wish to go on. Or maybe the coven members feel that it would be better for the initiate not to go on. I have known cases where to continue would have been both mentally and physically damaging to the person concerned. In cases of this sort, it is better to part in love and sorrow at losing a member than to allow them to go on.

When the initiate feels they no longer wish to continue, a vow of silence is put on them and they are formally released from their oath. They leave in friendship, on the understanding that they will have no contact with the coven again.

The case of one who wishes to go on but who is unsuited to the faith, for the reasons stated, is perhaps the saddest thing of all. They have to be eased out gently and banished from the circle. Not only that; it has to be explained why it is being done, with as little hurt as possible. If the coven so chooses, they can keep a discreet eye on that person and, should they ever need help, support them. It is not their fault that they did not make the grade. Because they tried, we owe it to them, and we always look after our own.

In the case of the initiate who, after taking what is a solemn oath, breaks it, the harsh and dark side of the faith comes into play. If we always look after our own, we should be allowed to defend our own. As a penance for minor breaches of coven rules, the offender is banned from as many meetings as the coven deems necessary. This is to be pronounced by the Lady and recorded by the Officer of the East in the coven records.

Where the initiate does deliberate harm to one of the members of the coven, or in the event of the deliberate revealing of any member's name to an outsider, or the revealing of the inner workings of a rite, the punishment must be banishment. The person concerned is brought before the coven, and the sword of judgment is carried into the circle. The Lady herself pronounces the ritual of expulsion. The person must be informed of the date when this is to take place; and even if they refuse to attend, the rite is still done.

Finally, the Officer of the East of the coven concerned must either himself or through the Summoner inform all the covens within the clan that this has been done. Also, the event must be entered into the clan records held by the senior coven.

After serving the year-and-a-day's apprenticeship, the initiate takes the full oath of membership in their own name. At this time, the initiate can reaffirm the use of their coven name or adopt another which they would like to be known by. The name, date and time of taking the oath are noted by East in the coven records and also passed on for entry in the clan records of the senior coven.

The Man in Black

To maintain contact between covens is the duty of the Man in Black. He is an enigmatic figure and one who is always a member of the parent coven. His token of office is the raven's feather, which should be worn unobtrusively when calling on the Lady of the coven in question. The function of this office is to observe, inform and report.

Sometimes circumstances call for the working of all the covens within the tradition, to a certain end. It is his duty to inform the Ladies of the covens concerned of the date, time and aim of the ritual that is being worked. It is the duty of each Lady to pass out the summons to all her coven members.

In his capacity as the Man in Black, he is entitled to attend any coven meeting within the clan. He may, if he so wishes, take part in the rites or stand apart and to the north during the ritual. At the feast afterwards, any new members are introduced to him by name, but he is always left unnamed. All questions and requests for aid are channelled back through him, and all replies come back through him also.

The final function of this office is to report back to the main coven anything of interest which has happened.

This is so that East may keep an accurate account of it in the clan records. His visit will be shown in the records of the coven concerned. At the same time, any questions or requests can be dealt with by the main coven and the answers passed back through him. Where contact has to be made over some distance, the Lady (or, if the coven desires to appoint one, the Summoner) will have his address and perhaps a telephone number and will contact him to raise any matter she feels is important enough to warrant it.

In most cases these matters fall into certain categories: to announce the name of anyone being banished, so that they can be struck off the records, and the rest of the clan be warned against them, or in the case of a need of healing or supporting any member in trouble. Finally, there is the matter of laying-on of a curse to protect any coven or member having trouble with some other person or group of persons. This is not something that is undertaken lightly, because a price will have to be paid for it. Yet at the same time, we must be prepared to defend our own.

The other rule or law concerning the Man in Black is that when he is on clan business he can claim food and shelter from the coven for the duration of his call. Usually some member is in a position to offer him hospitality, and he contributes something towards the cost of food.

The Summoner

The Summoner, as mentioned above, is one of those offices which, though not being critical to the running of the coven, is a good thing to have. On the one hand, an additional office gives members more to do in the running of the coven, and perhaps a new one may be appointed every year. On the other hand, the Summoner is a help to East, the record-keeper of the coven, to be able to leave the calling-out of members to someone else. The Summoner can also verify that the records being kept are true records, and if the coven so desires, he can sign as a witness to that effect.

Another job that very often falls to the Summoner is fixing up the transport to and from the meeting, as well as making sure with the Officer of the East that everything needed for the ritual gets to the working site. The fewer cars needed to get people from the gathering point to the site, the better. So it is up to the Summoner to see that any cars used are full.

Before the last part of the journey on foot to the site, the Summoner sees that everything needed is ready to go, and makes sure that it does so when everyone moves off to the site. His other task is to make sure that everything comes back that should come back, and he is the last one to leave the working area. It is surprising the number of times someone has had to go back for something, such as a forgotten knife.

As mentioned before, the Summoner is also the one to maintain contact with the Man in Black. He meets him and takes him to where everyone will assemble before the meeting, and later performs the introduction of new members to him.

As I have said previously, this is not a vital post within the coven, as these duties are usually associated with East. However, the office of Summoner is part of the old tradition, and as such it is a pleasant thing to have within the group. Also, having someone to deal with all the practical things which have to be done before a meeting does make life easier for everyone.

2   Coven Oaths

The Initiation Oath

This oath is always administered to the initiate in the circle
before the beginning of any of the rituals. The only
exception to this is at Hallowe'en, when due to the
differing nature of the rite, no one is ever initiated into the
circle. If the need should arise to initiate someone in time
for Hallowe'en, it is done in the same manner but at a
special ceremony.

As part of the oath, the initiate carries a small candle, the
soul candle, into the circle. Once in the circle, it is East
who speaks first:

East: 'Who sponsors this candidate?'

Sponsor: 'I [giving their coven name] do.'

East: 'Has what is about to be placed on him/her been
explained to him/her fully?'

Sponsor: 'It has. This I have done myself.'

East then speaks to the candidate:

East: 'Do you fully understand this oath that you are about
to take, and all that it involves?'

Candidate: 'I do so understand.'

East: 'Do you of your own free will choose to take this
oath?'

Candidate: 'I do so, freely and of my own accord.'

East: 'Then kneel before me and light your soul candle
from the fire.'

The candidate does this, and holds it in both hands.

East: 'Do you swear to serve the full year and a day as an
initiate?'

Candidate: 'I do so and of my own free will.'

East: 'Do you swear to hold all the coven workings as

sacred, and never reveal them to any outsider?'
Candidate: 'I do so and of my own free will.'
East: 'Do you swear never to reveal the name of any other coven member to anyone outside this gathering?'
Candidate: 'I do so and of my own free will.'
East: 'Do you swear to hold true to all the laws and rules of this coven?'
Candidate: 'I do so and of my own free will.'
East: 'Do you swear to renounce all other faiths and callings; to devote yourself to the ideals, aims and worship of the Mother; to hold true to the faith and these your chosen comrades?'
Candidate: 'I do so swear, by my very soul.'
East: 'Then repeat after me: "I [name] do solemnly swear to bind myself by this oath ... to call on the Old Ones to witness and note my swearing ... I promise to hold firm to this my oath with my very soul itself ... Should I break this my given word, may the Dark Gods of the Underworld strike me down ... and extinguish the very light of my existence ... as I do now with this candle, the symbol of my past life." '
The candle is extinguished accordingly. Then East speaks:
East: 'Take you now a new light from this our fire. For it is a symbol of your new life, your chosen one, one that you have freely selected and freely entered into. May the spirit that brought you to us stay with you, and be the light of inspiration within you for the rest of your days. Now rise, for the Lady of the circle waits to greet you.'
The candidate rises and with the candle still alight goes to the Lady, who is waiting in her usual position in the circle, in the north. Kneeling once more, the candidate places the candle on the ground to one side, and their hands between those of the Lady.
Candidate: 'Lady, I pledge myself to this our coven; to you, and all the others of our gathering. In my chosen name [candidate gives it], I swear to serve this our circle and all that it means and stands for. By my honour, I do so pledge.'
Lady: 'Then rise, brother/sister [giving the coven name], and join our congregation. For now you are truly one of us.'
Initiate: 'Lady, in love I came. In love I joined. In love I stay.

For this my pledge is given to gain my place within the circle.'

The Lady helps the initiate to their feet and, while having hold of their hands, kisses them on both cheeks.

Lady: 'Go join those who await you, so that we may tread the Mill and work our ways together.'

Initiate: 'As you so command, Lady.'

He or she bows and joins the others round the fire. They make way for the initiate and join hands ready to start the rite, which the Lady opens with the Sangreal Prayer.

The Oath of Full Membership

This is not so much an oath of membership as a reaffirmation by the person taking it in the aims, ideals and tenets of the faith as practised by the clan. It is also a recognition by the member that, by the taking of this oath, he or she is willing to accept the responsibilities that are part and parcel of the running of a coven. For instance, willingness to hold office within that coven and, finally, to advance the interests of the faith within the clan by starting a group of their own, within the framework of the system.

Once again, this oath is taken in the circle before the start of the ritual. As the date of the oath-taking is known beforehand, it is the duty of East to ensure that the coven sword is taken into the circle and put carefully to one side. Instead of the Lady's taking her usual place to the north, she stands by the sacred fire, with the membership forming a circle around her. She is the one to open the proceedings.

Lady: 'One of us is now ready to take the oath of fellowship. I call on each and every one of you to bear witness to this swearing, and that it be truly done by the laws of our gathering. I now call on the Lord of the East to bring forth the Sword of Justice, that this oath may be taken upon it.'

East brings the sword to the Lady. She unsheaths it and hands the scabbard back to East. He then returns to his position in the circle.

Lady: 'I call on our brother/sister [coven name] to

announce in front of all that are gathered here that [he/she] takes this oath of his/her own free will.'

Candidate: 'I do so state, Lady, and that I freely enter into all the obligations that the taking of this oath entails.'

Lady: 'Then I call upon my sister, the Lady of the South, to cast her girdle around the neck of brother/sister [coven name] and lead him/her forth to me.'

South: 'As you so command, Lady.'

South, holding her waist cord in her hand, approaches the candidate. Forming a loop in the cord by holding both ends in the one hand, she slips it over the candidate's head.

South: 'By this halter shall you be led to the destiny of your own making. You chose to heed the call that led you to our circle. Now I lead you to your final commitment.'

With the cord still looped around the candidate's neck, South leads them to the Lady.

South: 'Lady, as commanded I bring before you [name], to take this the final pledge.'

She hands the ends of the cord to the Lady and returns to her position. The Lady, with the sword in her right hand and the cord in her left, holds out the blade point-first to the candidate and commands them to kneel and take the blade in both hands.

Lady: 'Repeat these words after me: "I [name], do solemnly swear by all that I hold sacred, to obey the laws and uphold the spirit of this our coven. To hold true to the faith and all that it entails. To commit myself fully to serving and aiding all others in the congregation. To accept office willingly, and to discharge the duties of that office to the best of my ability. To serve the coven, and through the coven the Lady, with all my heart and soul. To accept the disciplines that the faith places on me, so that the manner and rhythms of our worship shall not be disturbed by any animosity brought within the circle. Once again I call upon the Lady and the Old Gods to witness this my oath. Should I knowingly break it, then I stand ready to be judged by the sword, and by the sword accept the banishment and all that it entails, as my just due. In the name of Our Lady of the Night, I do so swear." '

After the candidate has finished repeating the oath, the Lady tells them to rise. She kisses the candidate on both cheeks as a sign of acceptance.

Lady: 'Welcome to our congregation. For by the taking of this oath, you have become one of us.'

The Lady then calls on South with the words:

Lady: 'My Lady of the South, lead this our new brother/sister back to his/her place within the congregation.'

South: 'As you so command, Lady.'

Before turning to the new member, South receives her cord back from the Lady, re-tying it around her waist. She turns to the new member and holds out her right hand to them. At the same time she kisses them on both cheeks.

South: 'As I brought you to the Lady by the halter, so I take you back to your place by the hand. By the joining of hands we symbolize the joining of all within the circle.'

She then leads the new member back to their place.

The final part of the ceremony is when the Lady calls upon East to take back the coven sword. He does so, returning it to its scabbard and then taking it back to a safe place before taking up his position again.

The Lady leaves the circle of members and returns to her usual position in the north. She turns to face the gathering, with the words:

Lady: 'Let the rite begin.'

She then signals the start of the ritual by repeating the Sangreal Prayer.

The Oath of Office

With the taking of the oath of office, the person having put themselves forward for selection takes on added duties and burdens in the name of the coven. The strength of any coven lies in the character of the people running it. Bad officers, unhappy coven; good officers, happy coven. So before anyone considers standing for office, they must be sure within themselves that they are doing it for all the right reasons, rather than for self-aggrandizement or an exercise of power for their own ends. An officer must be a leader in the true sense of the word. So, before standing, the person concerned should ask themself a few questions before taking on the responsibilities involved:

What are my reasons for wanting office? Am I doing it for myself or to advance the interests of the clan through my efforts?

Have I the patience, understanding and tolerance needed to discharge that office?

Have I the inner strength and calmness needed to be fair and objective in decisions that I am called upon to make in the name of the coven or clan?

Am I willing to undertake these duties for seven years, and have I the strength of purpose to stand down if I feel within myself that I am failing to discharge those duties as they should be discharged?

Once again this oath is taken within the circle; but instead of its being taken before a ritual, as with the other oath-takings, it is taken when the maximum number of members can be gathered together on a date to be decided by the Lady. Instead of the membership's gathering inside the circle, they space themselves out around the perimeter. The only people inside the circle are the Lady and the existing officers.

As this is a ceremony and not a ritual, the circle is laid out in the usual manner but omitting the dedication and the calling on the gods to guard the sacred area. If East is one of the existing officers, he will bring the coven sword into the circle with him. If East is the officer to be sworn in, it is carried in by West or the Lady.

As there is no magical purpose to this rite, the broom or besom which forms the bridge is left in position for the new officer to cross into the circle. The Lady takes her position by the fire, with the other officers gathered behind her. Once again, she opens the proceedings with the Sangreal Prayer:

Beloved Bloodmother of my especial breed,
Welcome me at this moment with your willing womb.
Let me learn to live in love with all you are,
So my seeking spirit serves the Sangreal.

There is a pause of a few moments, for the congregation to take into themselves some of the solemnity of the occasion. The Lady then continues:

Lady: 'I call on brother/sister [name] to enter the circle and stand before me.'

The new officer does so, going to each quarter in turn, starting with the east, and calling on the spirit of that quarter by name, using an invocation of their own composing. Having done this, they go over to the Lady and face her.

Lady: 'You have put your name forward to hold office within our coven. By the consent of the congregation, I am empowered to call you to that office.'

Candidate: 'That is so, Lady, and I stand before you to receive that office from your hands.'

Lady: 'For the final time of asking, and in the presence of all, I ask you once again. Are you willing to hold that said office and discharge the same according to the tenets of our faith?'

Candidate: 'I am willing so to do, Lady.'

Lady: 'Then kneel before me and, taking the blade of the Sword of Justice in both your hands, repeat this oath after me.'

The candidate does so, bowing his or her head to the Lady in homage.

Lady: 'I [name] do swear in the name of the Mother, Our Lady of the Night ... and by the faith that I hold dear to my heart ... that of my own free will and by the call I feel within myself ... I do accept willingly the obligations placed upon me by the holding of this office of [title] ... That I shall discharge the functions of that office humbly and properly, with due respect to Our Lady and Her Horned Consort and Son ... That I shall work within the traditions of our clan, to further the aims of our fellowship and to be a true guide to all those who choose to enter our sacred ring ... I also pledge that if through no fault of my own I should be found wanting, or feel unable to carry out the duties of that office ... I shall cheerfully stand down and let another fill my place ... For the honour of office is not for myself ... but for the honouring of Our Lady, Queen of the Heavens ... By all that I hold sacred and by my very soul itself ... I swear to stand true to this my oath ... For I seek not to take the power, but to receive it from whence it is given ... I call upon the Lady of the high and lonely places to witness this my oath, and call upon her to help me be true to it.'

Passing the sword to one of the officers behind her, the Lady then calls on the new officer to stand up. She moves close enough to the new officer to be able to touch him or her, and then speaks:

Lady: 'From my breast to thy breast.' With her right hand she touches her breast and then the breast of the new officer.

Lady: 'From my thigh to thy thigh.'

With the same hand she touches her thigh and then the thigh of the new officer, before continuing:

Lady: 'I transfer some of the power granted to me by right of office to you, our new Lord/Lady of the [title].

New officer: 'I thank you, Lady, with all my heart, and pray that I shall be worthy of this office.'

Lady: 'One more thing remains to be done. Once more I ask you to kneel before me.'

The new officer does so. One of the existing officers pours a cup of wine, which they then hand to the Lady. She offers the cup to the kneeling officer, with the words:

Lady: 'Come, join me in this token feast that is special to just you and me.'

The new officer drinks half the wine and then hands the cup back to the Lady for her to finish. She does so and hands the cup back to the officer who gave it to her. He or she in turn hands the Lady a piece of bread, which she breaks in half. Handing one piece to the kneeling officer, she says:

Lady: 'Eat of the bread that I have broken before you. For this is our private feast, a token of the mystic union that joins me to thee.'

Both eat the bread, and when they have finished, the Lady holds out both her hands to help the new officer rise. She then kisses him or her on both cheeks in welcome.

The final part of the ceremony takes place when the Lady, holding the new officer by the hand and with the other officers following, goes first to the north, and then following the perimeter of the circle round to the east, she performs a ritual showing of the new officer to the congregation.

After this has been done, she helps everyone over the bridge and closes the circle by removing the broomstick or besom. The usual procedure then is for a party to be thrown, to celebrate the installation of the new Lord or Lady of the quarter, East, South, West or North. As is usual for these parties, everyone brings some food or drink for the sharing.

The Oath for the Lady

In some ways this is a misnomer, as what the Lady actually does is to open herself to the Mother as well as taking the oath of office. On the one hand, she is pledging herself to lead the coven. On the other, she is calling on the Goddess to join with her in a mystic union of soul to spirit. Unless there is that joining (known in other traditions as 'the Inner Plane contact'), the workings of the coven will seem flat and empty. For she is the bridge, the link between the Goddess and the congregation. To her, through her and from her, the power flows to the gathering. So she has to be a very strong-willed person to handle it.

It is said that Ladies (or High Priestesses as they are called in some other traditions) are born, not made; and in some ways I agree. No one stands for this office just because they feel like it. They are called to it by the Mother herself.

So how to arrive at a suitable candidate from within the group or coven? In the first instance, the coven members are polled on their views by the officers. After one or more names have been put forward, the officers fix a date to meet within a circle cast for the purpose. Partly by discussion and partly by inspiration, the name of the Lady becomes known. It is then the duty of East to approach the chosen one and obtain her agreement to the selection. On her agreement, a date is set by the officers for a full gathering of all members, so that they are informed and introduced to the new Lady.

At this meeting, a time must be set for her to take the oath of office, and set far enough into the future to give the Lady time to prepare herself. Usually the oath-taking is held fourteen days after the introduction. This time-gap will also give a newly formed group or coven a chance to get some small piece of silver jewellery to be used as a badge or token of office. For myself, I think a pair of silver bracelets is ideal, as they can be passed on to every new Lady of the coven when the need arises. As mentioned before, the Lady must either renew her oath, using the same rite, at the end of seven years, or stand down. In this case, the new Lady receives the bracelets as a badge of office at her oath-taking, or the old Lady is re-invested with them when she retakes the oath.

The circle is cast as usual by East. But instead of his leaving the circle and then receiving the staff from the Lady to set it up, he takes the staff himself, sets it up and then returns to the circle. (He must do this as, at that moment, technically, the coven has no Lady.)

Then, going to each quarter in turn, starting at the east and bowing low, he invokes the aspect of that quarter with the words:

East: 'I call upon the spirit of the [naming the quarter] to be with us and to bear witness to this our act of worship.'

He then goes to the fire and uses the rite of dedication of the circle (see pp.150–4). His next move is to return to the bridge and help into the circle the other three officers in turn, and then the rest of the gathering. When everyone is in the circle, North closes it by bringing in the broom and leaving it close to the edge of the circle. She then returns to the others, who have formed up in the shape of a horseshoe round the sacred fire, with the open end facing to the north. The Lady who is about to take the oath goes to her position, in the north and just inside the circle's edge, waiting for the summons from East for her to join the congregation.

As in the case of the oath of membership, the Lady swears by the coven sword. In her case, however, the blade of the sword is not proffered to her for the oath-swearing. Instead, she actually holds the weapon by the hilt with the blade pointing upwards, while making her pledge. Once again, it is East who has wardship of the coven sword, while the bracelets are in the care of the Ladies of the North and South. The cup and wine are in

the charge of the Lord of the West. When all is ready, East
speaks:
East: 'Brothers and sisters, tonight from within our ranks
we will have a Lady. One of our own choosing, who will
pledge before us all to serve the Goddess, and to lead this
our coven in her worship … I now call upon that Lady to
join us.'

She does so, making her way between the congregation
until she is close to and facing the Officer of the East.
East: 'Lady, accept from me in the name of the Goddess,
this sword, that you may take your oath upon it.'
Lady: 'This I am willing to do.'
    She takes the unsheathed sword from East by the hilt.
First touching the point on the ground and then holding it
blade upwards, she makes her vow:
Lady: 'As this sword touched first the earth and then
pointed to the heavens … So I pledge that I too shall act as
a true bridge between Our Lady and her congregation …
To act in all fairness and favour none … To bring harmony
to those of our fellowship, that we may truly be a
gathering of like minds … To be a true aid to those who
seek to find the path of enlightenment … To listen with
both heart and mind to what is said by others … To look
beyond the veil that hides our mysteries, and to help
others to do the same … To serve this congregation
through the office of Lady … And above all, to be true to
the Goddess and all she stands for … and to lead our
coven in her worship … By this sword and by my soul … I
pledge to do so.'

The Lady kisses the blade and hands back the sword to
East. East then calls forward the Ladies of North and
South to present the tokens of office. In silence they
approach the Lady, who extends her arms for them to
fasten the bracelets on her wrists. When this is done, they
bow to her and return to their places. East then speaks:
East: 'From your two sisters you have received the tokens
of your office. Remember that you wear them for us all,
and in our name act as Lady of this coven.'
Lady: 'My Lord of the East, I pledge to remember it well;
and should I forget, I call on each and every one of you to
remind me of my pledge. And at the end of my seven

years of office, I stand ready to be judged upon my merits by all of you, before the retaking of this my oath.'

It is then the turn of the Lord of the West to step forward and offer the Lady the cup of wine, with the words:

West: 'Lady, I offer you this cup, a symbol of the Cauldron of Inspiration. The wine held within it is symbolic of the wisdom and knowledge that is contained within the cauldron. As you drink deeply of this wine, may you drink as deeply from the cauldron, so that some measure of that wisdom will be passed on to us, through the grace of Our Lady and all that she stands for.'

Lady: 'I thank you, my Lord of the West, and pray that the symbol shall become fact and that the scales of darkness fall from our eyes and we see clearly the path that we have chosen to tread.'

The Lady holds the cup up at arm's length above her head and calls upon the Mother by using the Sangreal Prayer:

Beloved Bloodmother of my especial breed,
Welcome me at this moment with your willing womb.
Let me learn to live in love with all you are,
So that my seeking spirit serves the Sangreal.

She drains the cup and turns it upside down to show that it is empty. The Lady then hands it back to West with these words:

Lady: 'I have drunk deeply of the wine, and now pray that what I have done symbolically may become reality, and that a goodly measure of wisdom may be granted to me. In the Mother's name, I do so ask.'

East then addresses the congregation.

East: 'Our Lady has now taken the pledge to serve us. We too in turn must pledge ourselves to serve her. As agreed by all, and in the name of all, I shall lead us in doing so.'

The congregation then kneels. East approaches the Lady and kneels too. She takes both his hands between hers.

East: 'In the name of Our Lady the Mother, and on behalf of all ... I pledge to serve you faithfully, in thought, in

word, in deed ... To uphold the dignity of your office ... and to obey all lawful instructions, according to the tenets of our faith ... To seek through serving you, to serve the Mother, Our Lady, and all that she stands for ... In truth, honesty and sincerity, on behalf of us all, I do so pledge.'
Coven: 'In Our Lady's name, so be it done.'
Lady: 'Your fealty I accept as owing to the Mother. In her name, it is so taken.'

All rise and bow to the Lady. She returns the greeting by crossing her arms on her breast and bowing back. She returns to her position in the north and, by placing the besom across the edge of the circle, reopens the gateway to the outside world. East then leads everyone out of the circle.

The Lady, instead of leaving the circle, closes it behind them and returns to the sacred fire. The congregation goes some distance away, leaving the Lady within the circle.

What transpires then is between the Goddess and the Lady. This is the time when the special pact or bond is made between them, and it is certainly nothing to do with any other member of the coven. The only thing the gathering has to do is to wait for her to leave what is now *her* circle, when she feels ready to do so.

A party can be held in celebration afterwards, and as usual each member brings a little food and drink for the sharing by all.

III   Tools and Regalia

1   The Working Tools

In most religions there are certain vessels and articles which take on a sacred and ritual meaning and usage. The Craft as such is no stranger to these ideas. In fact, as a faith that had to go underground for a long period of time, it is particularly rich in sacred artefacts.

Because of the dangers inherent in the possession of the tools, most of them were of a common or household nature. But irrespective of this, they were and still are of a religious nature that is rich in symbolic meaning and usage. So a look must now be taken at the more common tools and their meaning and usage within the faith.

The tools can be broadly divided into two categories, namely those which are personal to the individual witch, and those which are owned by the coven. In the case of the individual, the basic tools are firstly, the knife; secondly, the cord; thirdly, the stang. In the case of the coven, there are six tools; namely, the cup, the knife, the altar stang, the besom, the sword and the cauldron. The cauldron is optional, mainly because of the difficulty of getting a suitable one in good enough condition to be used. But at the same time, a cauldron is a nice thing to have; and if a permanent home can be found for it to be set up, it will form part of the altar regalia.

So, starting with the personal tools and then progressing to the coven tools, we will take a brief look at each tool in turn, and their meaning and usage as peculiar to the Craft. As these uses are described in basic form only, further research into them can and should be done. Research of this nature is rewarding to both individual and coven, and to the faith as a whole.

The Knife

As held by the individual, this is a symbol of will. As a tool, it has the ability to direct that will in the form of magical energy. During private workings, it is used as a focal point for concentration during the treading of the Dance of the Mill, and as a pointer for the directing of that energy when raised. When used in this context, it serves the same purpose as the magician's wand or sword.

The other aspect that it takes on is sexual in nature, and as a phallic symbol it is used in the dedication of the wine. At full coven meetings, this is done with the coven knife; but in the course of working with a partner and in the monthly rites, whether they are worked by a small group within the coven or just a working couple, the knife of the officiating pair is used.

Because of the fertility aspect of the Old Faith, it is incompatible with nature and with the creation of life that one person can consecrate the wine within the cup. Apart from virgin birth, life can be created only by the man's entering the woman and fertilizing the ovum within her. So it is with the wine in the cup. Only by the symbolizing of the sexual act can the wine be changed from being just wine into a mystically enhanced fluid, containing a small portion of the wisdom of the sacred cauldron, which the cup represents. The lowering of the knife into the wine-cup, which is held by the woman, symbolizes the joining of male and female in the act of creation, thus charging the cup with life and with the wisdom of the ages which is contained within that life.

On a more practical level, the knife is used to mark out or trace the working circle, on both coven and individual levels. In this guise, when working outside, it becomes the equivalent of the plough. Throughout ancient history, the founding of a new city was marked by the ploughing of the boundary delineating the limits of that city. This was always done in a deeply reverential and religious manner, calling on the gods to recognize the boundary and to aid, favour and protect all that dwelt within the boundary line.

The same is asked when marking out or tracing the perimeter of the circle. After it has been marked out, the gods and goddesses are invoked to be 'Likened unto a wall of stone around this our circle's edge and to protect all that are within'. When used for this purpose, the knife becomes *de facto* the sacred iron-shod plough which either creates a sacred boundary or destroys one, as in the case of the ancient city of Carthage – the Romans ritually ploughed the site of this city and formally cursed it by sowing it with salt.

On another level, the knife is used in the manner in which a knife should be used, namely for cutting things. When the individual finds the wood for his or her stang growing in the woods, tradition has it that this should be cut with a ritual knife. When greenery is cut for the garland on the staff, once again the ritual knife is used. It is also used for cutting food at the feast after any ritual. In short, it is a commonplace article which in the past would incite no comment concerning the owner of it. In fact, everyone would be expected to have one.

Traditionally, the knife is the black-handled athame which is consecrated by the owner and is particular to that person alone. Also by tradition, each male member of the coven should forge his own knife, while the female members should have theirs forged by their working partner or by a skilled member of the coven. Unfortunately, today people who have the necessary skills to forge and temper a blade are few and far between, and to buy a hand-forged knife is very costly. I know this because one of the knives I have is hand-forged. It was given to me on loan for this lifetime. If I had had to buy it, it would have cost me $400, and the blade is only four inches long. The first ritual knife I had was an old hunting-knife. It was ritually cleansed and then dedicated for me by the master of our coven. In this, I was lucky that he was willing to do it for me. In the case of most people, they get hold of a knife they feel happy with and dedicate it themselves.

This being so, just what are the aim and theology behind the dedication of the knife?

(1) To cleanse the blade from its past history. To remove all secular influences that went into the making of it. To present it at its dedication as being clean and empty of all influences, ready to be recharged with magical power.

This cleansing is done ritually in the name of the four elements – earth, air, fire and water.

(2) To charge the knife magically with some of the power raised in the circle. To instil into that knife some of your own identity and personality, so that the knife becomes part of you, and through you part of your will which manifests itself through the knife. A magical tool that is an extension of your arm, with the point as the focus of energy raised to a particular end. In short, the knife becomes a physical expression of part of your soul, as within the aura of that knife part of the soul has been transferred. An oath sworn by the knife is synonymous with the swearing by the soul. To a true coven member they are one and the same thing.

Past civilizations set great store by the sacred nature of the blade. Hence the recognition of the personality of certain blades, and the naming of them, giving them a certain life of their own (King Arthur's sword Excalibur, for instance). If anyone feels the urge to personalize their knife with a name, there is no better title for it than the first magical act it performs after dedication.

The rites for the cleansing and dedication of the knife, as for all the other tools, will be given later on.

The one thing that must be remembered is that the knife is a sacred tool, and as such it should be treated with reverence and respect. The knife has its place within the faith and at the foot of the altar, and should be shown the respect that is due to it. When a witch dies, the knife is either buried with them or destroyed. Once dedicated to the service of the Goddess, it should never be used for any non-sacred task. Cutting food at the feast is part of any ritual, so its use in this sense is part of that ritual too.

One note of warning: the drawn knife should never be used as a focal point of concentration during any full coven meeting. Otherwise, some night someone will be concentrating on the blade while pacing the Mill, when the person in front stops unexpectedly – and you'll have an involuntary sacrifice on your hands! Bare blades are better kept out of the full circle and confined to those occasions when there are just two people working together.

The Cord

The cord as part of the personal regalia is very often used to mark the rank or degree of the wearer within the coven. This is of course a matter for individual covens within the clan system to decide on. For my own personal feelings, I prefer to stick to two colours of cord as used by the membership. In the case of initiates, a red one is used. On taking the full oath of membership, this is exchanged for a black one. If any coven or group within the system wishes to include the changing of cords as part of the oath-taking, there is no earthly reason why it should not be done this way. The one thing that must be remembered is that any colours used for degrees within any coven or group are effective only within that group and will bear no weight or authority within any other coven of the clan.

In the case of the Lady and other officers of the coven, this again is a matter for the group to decide what they feel is right. Once again on a personal level, I think that the most appropriate colours for the officers are as follows: silver for the Lady, yellow or orange for East, gold or bright yellow for South, black or dark brown for West, black or white or even a combination of the two for North. But once again I must stress that this choice must be up to the individual covens, because what is meaningful for one coven may not be as meaningful to another coven or group within the clan.

One thing that always seems to raise some controversy is the number of knots which should be tied in the cord. Some claim that the correct number is thirteen, while others claim that the number should be nine. In the case of thirteen knots, these equal the number of members in a full coven, as well as being the number of months in the lunar or synodic year. The number nine or three-times-three has always had a magical significance. But once again I feel that it is up to the individual to knot into the cord the thoughts and influences they feel belong within it.

In my own case, I always use nine knots, and each one was tied with a memory from the past. Using it as a form of rosary, it reminds me of some specific act or deed connected with something done within the circle. As a couple of these proved with hindsight to be mistakes, the two knots tied for them remind me to think before acting. Not a bad motto for any working occultist to bear in mind.

One of the questions that was asked of me in my early days was, 'Where does a witch wear the garter?' The answer was, 'Around their neck.' Why around the neck? In the taking of the oath of full membership, the Officer of the South loops her cord around the neck of the candidate, to lead them to the Lady. In this case, the cord becomes a halter. This action got me thinking; so for what it is worth, I advance my own theory for consideration. The cord as such is nothing more nor less than a ritual garotte.

In the first instance, we must take a look at and try to understand the ancient mentality which enabled a person to volunteer as a sacrifice. Today we find it hard to understand how a person could choose to die in this way. I suppose that finding enough faith to accept the fate of a messenger to the gods does seem rather hard to understand. Yet in the past many early cultures considered this certainty of belief to be the norm rather than the exception.

I know that in some cases it is thought that prisoners or slaves were used. But in many cases the victims were willing to accompany a great leader or king into the grave. As an example of this, one only has to look at the reports of the excavation of the Royal Cemetery of Ur of the Chaldees. The bodies found in the burial pit were definitely not slaves forced to die in this way but willing volunteers. One point that should be noted is the lack of grave goods with the bodies. This leads to the conclusion that the people themselves were considered as grave goods belonging to the king, a retinue that still served him beyond the grave.

With the commercial exploitation of peat bogs, more and more ancient bodies are being discovered. Because of the chemical action of bog water, the corpses found are in a near-perfect state of preservation. Bodies found as far apart as Denmark, Ireland and Britain show signs not only of having been ritually killed but of having in common that each one had been strangled, and the knotted cord used had been left in position. Whether or not these were willing sacrifices can never be established; but the common factor is that they were all ritually strangled.

For an eyewitness report on the use of a garotte in a human sacrifice, a leap forward in time from the date of the peat-bog victims must be taken, to about AD 922. We owe this description to the Arab traveller Ibn Fadlan, whose curiosity led him to witness the funeral rites of a Swedish chieftain of the Volga region. Without going too deeply into the story, the two salient factors to be noted are, firstly, the asking of all the dead man's female slaves or servants which one of them was willing to die for their master. Secondly, after a series of complicated rituals, the volunteer was handed over to the Old Hag – also known as the Angel of Death – and her two daughters.

As the final part of the ritual, the priestess playing the part of the Angel of Death led the girl into the tent which had been erected over the body of the chief. Her entry into it was a signal for all the men present to beat on their shields with sticks. Six close friends of the dead man then entered the tent and had sexual intercourse with her. After this, she was placed next to the body, with two men holding her legs and two holding her arms. The Old Hag or the Angel of Death looped a cord round the girl's throat and handed the ends to the last two men. While they were pulling the ends of the cord, she stabbed the girl between the ribs with a broad-bladed knife. Once again, the cord is an instrument of death for a willing sacrifice. Also, there is the fact that the Angel of Death was the one who had charge of the cord. In the coven, she is the Lady of the North, the Pale-Faced One who presides over the cauldron.

So with the cord we see the dark and cruel side of the Old Faith: the priesthood of the tribe sacrificing for the good of the tribe. The strangulation of the victim was only one part of the full ceremony; but as with all things, time modifies the concept. Even though the sacrifice of the Divine King was no longer practised, the instrument of sacrifice became part of the regalia of the faith.

Bearing in mind the idea of the sacrificed messenger to the Goddess, the symbology behind the leading-forth of the full member by the Lady of the South at the oath-taking, by using her cord as a halter, is one that expresses the acceptance of the fate which is placed on a full member. The leading-forth is a pseudo-death at the feet of the Goddess, as represented by the Lady. The returning by the hand is a stylized form of rebirth, and all that is involved by the taking of the oath. One is reborn within the clan of one's choosing. That is why some members choose to use another name after taking the oath. By going through a pseudo-death, they are returning as a different person, a symbolic rebirth within the coven.

If the coven has decided that different-coloured cords are to be used to distinguish the initiate from the full member, this is the time when the cords are exchanged. This exchanging of cords can be made as simple or as complicated as the coven desires. In fact, one idea that has been put forward for consideration is that the initiates' cords are held by the coven and issued to them by the coven. When the initiate takes the full oath of membership, a knot is tied into the cord to commemorate the event, and it is then passed on to a new initiate. When a full thirteen knots have been tied, the cord can be laid up as part of the coven regalia. The passing of the cord from one initiate to another in this way means that a small part of the coven history is built into the cord. In time, a magical power is gathered within the cord itself. This in turn is passed on from one user to the other.

Anything that helps to create a continuity within the framework of the clan and coven can only strengthen the bonds between individual members. Thus the many shall become as one in worship.

The Stang

Perhaps it would be more correct to say 'the stangs', on the grounds that there is more than one type of the same tool. There is the individual's stang, the coven stang and the blackthorn stang used in the cursing of the enemies of the clan, coven or group. The coven stang and the blackthorn stang with their different aspects, attributes and usage will be dealt with in the chapter devoted to the coven regalia, even though many of the attributes are common to both.

As with many of the craft tools, the origins of the stang are lost in the mists of time and history. The few hints that we do have of its early usage are really nothing more than speculation and conjecture, rather like those in Alfred Watkins' book *The Old Straight Track*. There are claims that his 'Men-of-the-Leys' or 'Dodmen', with their forked surveying sticks, have a common ancestry with the witches. This is a theory that it is impossible to prove or disprove. Yet at the same time it is a possibility, in the light of the tradition of witch connections with ancient trackways and in particular with crossroads, one of their traditional meeting-places. In fact, legend has it that many witches were buried at crossroads.

One of the few facts known for sure is that the forked or horned staff is peculiar to the craft. As an example of this, I can recall a visit to Stonehenge by a few of our group. Some of us had been on a visit to Salisbury Plain and had decided to see Stonehenge on the way home. At this particular time, I was the only one present with his own staff. In we went, with me using the stang as a walking-stick. At the cash desk, one of the attendants was heard to say to the other, 'He's a witch. That's a witch's stang he's got there.' A clear case of recognition by identification – the forked stang was the trademark.

So just what function should the stang fill on a personal level? As such, the stang is an emblem of faith, of belonging and acceptance of that faith and all that it entails. It serves as a personal 'altar' for the owner, as a walking-aid to and from meetings and also as a token or sign that one is of the craft. The most important of these functions is of course that of the altar.

In this concept, the stang represents the Divine God-King of the woodland glade, the god of hunting and fertility. Within this concept of a totem emblem falls the sacrificial rite of the killing of the Divine King-Priest of the May Eve rituals, to release the spirit of summer; for instance, the release of Jack-in-the-Green, symbolized by a dancing bush that is pushed over to 'kill' it. In the Tree-God aspect, it is the sanctified Oak-King served by

Robin Goodfellow or Robin Hood, with Maid Marian and eleven others making the full coven of thirteen. Also it is symbolic of the Horned Consort-child of the Goddess in the form of Diana of the Greenwoods, Diana Nemorensia. In this light, the owner of the altar staff becomes in a sense a descendant of the priest-king guardian of the sacred tree in the grove of Diana at Nemi.

As an individual working tool, the use of the staff can be made as simple or as complicated as one chooses. A couple joining together as working partners outside the main coven meetings should set up a stang as an altar. This can be done in two ways, and once again can be as simple or elaborate as desired. In the first case, and one that is suitable for outside workings or, if one has sufficient room, inside workings, the stang is set up as an altar in the centre of a circle.

Whether the rite is worked in or out of doors, a nine-foot circle is used, and the casting of the circle is modified slightly by the absence of the besom. Closing the circle is done from the inside by tracing the line through. If the rite is being done indoors, the stang can be mounted in a bucket of sand while the circle is traced out with a knife in a token manner. For those who have the room and intend to work inside a good deal, the best thing is to use a piece of canvas with the circle painted on it in white.

When the stang is mounted in the centre, a small candle is lit and fixed between the forks or horns. The cakes and wine are dedicated in the usual way, and the Dance of the Mill trodden either widdershins or deosil, depending on the purpose for which the rite is being worked.

At this stage, a look should be taken at the question of working in the nude. Once again, this is up to the people concerned. There is a tradition of working nude, and good magical reasons for doing so. As an indoor practice there is a lot to be said for it. On the other hand, being fat and forty is good enough reason for not doing so. The choice of working nude must be left to the individuals working together to decide. No one must ever be forced into it against their will.

In the case of a couple working together with insufficient room to set up the stang in the circle, or in the case of an individual working alone, the aims and methods are different from those of the circle rite. It is a ceremonial act rather than a practical working rite. Some people feel that once a month is an ideal time-scale, while others like to greet each new quarter separately and go as far as keeping a special calendar to celebrate the full synodic year. Without going to that extent, it is still nice to work a rite ceremonially, either on one's own or with a partner, outside the quarterly rites. In the ceremonial rituals, the stang, with the aid of a bucket of sand, is placed in a cleared area. Close up to it is a table; if lacking space, I have found that a small coffee table is ideal. On it will be candlesticks and candles, a small pot of sand with a couple of joss-sticks planted upright in it, a glass and a bottle of wine. In the case of a male–female couple, they – being able to consecrate both cakes and wine – would have the cakes and the knife on the table as well, to perform the dedication in the usual way.

The person working alone, being unable to consecrate both cakes and wine, would light the candle or candles and the joss-sticks and then use a rite of their own composition. When it is time for the wine to be poured, they fill the glass and raise it while at the same time saying:

'My Lady ... Goddess of the Night ... I pray that you both see and hear me ... For what I have done is in both your honour and your name ... I pray that you accept this act of worship, solitary though it may be ... And pray that I shall be granted the inner peace and knowledge that is the measure of your following ... Through that knowledge ... Gain wisdom to accept life as it is and to live it in love for what you are ... So that my searching spirit finds peace within your service ... I drain this glass in Our Lady's name and the memory of those whom I have known ... May they too share some of the things that I feel at this moment ... In Our Lady's name, I do so pray.'

The glass is drained and the ceremony ended.

One other point that should be noted is that the stang used as a personal altar is never garlanded as the coven staff is. If one feels the need for flowers on the altar, these should be presented as a posy or a solitary rose as a reminder of the Rose Beyond the Grave, and seen as an emblem of immortality.

'Seek and ye shall find' sums up rather neatly the job one has in finding a decent ash staff. The areas where the old art of coppicing is carried out today are few and far between. But when a staff is found, you will know if it is the one for you. It will feel right to the hand. A slight tingling in the fingers will tell you that it is yours and for you alone. Tradition has it that it should be cut during the full-moon period with one's own knife. As most forests with ash in them are so far out of town, most people will cut their staff during the day. However, there is one ritual which should never be overlooked, simple though it is. When something is taken, something must be left in its place. When taking the staff, a small coin is left behind as payment.

The next thing that needs to be looked at is the consecration of the stang. As with all personal tools, the consecration of the stang is done in the name of the four elements of earth, air, fire and water. But before doing this, the stang must be shod with iron. This is done by simply hammering a nail into the foot of it. As this is common to the coven stang as well, the reasons for doing it will be given later, in the chapter dealing with coven regalia.

Concerning the rite of consecration, this is usually done by the owner out of doors. Briefly, the stang is first passed through fire to purify it, then it is sprinkled with water. After this is done, the stang is planted upright in the element of earth. Next it is blown on three times, and finally the owner loops their cord around their wrist and the stang while invoking the Goddess in her aspect as the Mother ' ... to charge this staff with a portion of her powers and make it truly a magical tool'.

Once the stang is purified and consecrated, it must be remembered that it is no longer just another piece of ash wood. It is a magically charged working tool, an altar and a representation of the Horned God. In one aspect, it takes on the same ritual meaning as the Sacred Tree in the grove of Diana; while to a certain degree you take on the obligations of the priest-king of the sacred grove, and servant of both the Horned God and the Goddess herself.

Consecrating the Tools

As the same rite is used for all the personal tools, this section will be written using the consecration of the knife as an example. Only towards the end of the rite is there any difference, when dealing with the stang. These differences will be explained and dealt with at the end of the ritual. As these rites include the use of fire and water, they are perhaps better done out of doors.

The selection of time and place is up to the individual; or if a couple who work together are doing the consecration, it is done when they feel the time is right. To be strictly traditional about it, the rite should be done between the new- and full-moon phases. In a magical sense, the growing moon equates to a growing power. During the waning stages, the power is slowly ebbing, and the energy charging the knife or stang will be weaker. As to the validity of this belief, I would hesitate to pass judgment. Any tools which I have consecrated have always been done during the full-moon period. But, as I have said before, this is up to the individual concerned.

As is the practice for any magical working, the circle must be cast in the usual way. In the centre of it is the fire, the first of the elements to be used in the rite of consecration. The knife must be passed through the fire three times. Each time this is done, these words are used:

'Thus through the fires of purification I pass this knife, where both past and present are burnt from it.'

The next stage is to sprinkle the knife with the element of water three times, using these words each time:

'With the waters of time and forgetfulness I wash away the ashes of both past and present. Thus it is ready to serve a new purpose.'

Next the knife is planted in the element of earth, using the words:

'Thus I plant this knife in the earth, womb of the Mother. From the womb comes life, and that life when held within this blade shall have the power to charge the wine and to direct the energy raised within the circle.

Thus by the womb of the Mother, this blade becomes an instrument and focal point of my will.'

The final part of the rite is when the knife is withdrawn. In the name of the element of air, the knife is breathed on three times, using the words:

'By this breath, as life is breathed into us, so I breathe life into this my knife. By doing so, I breathe part of myself into this my blade. In the name of Our Lady, so shall it be.'

As noted before, in the main the rite for the stang follows the same pattern as that used for the knife. Where the two differ is when the stang is planted in the element of earth. In this case the words used are:

'The staff that I plant into the soil, by the powers of Our Lady the Goddess, shall be charged with the energy found within the circle, making this stang a true symbol of the altar of her creation. In her name I so declare it.'

The next step is to drive the nail into the foot of the stang, using these words:

'With this iron I close the end of this my stang, preserving within it the powers endowed upon it by Our Lady, Queen of the Heavens and of the Night. In her name I pray that she will make this stang a true symbol of her following. By her name, so be it done.'

The next step is to hold the stang in both hands and breathe three times upon it, using the words:

'As life is breathed into us, so I breathe life into this symbol of the Horned God, Child of Our Lady. Thus part of me is transferred into this my stang.'

The final part of the actual rite is the linking of the owner and the stang with the cord. This is looped round the stang and the ends held by the owner in the left hand. The words used for this part of the rite are:

'By the cord I join myself to this my stang, it being a symbol of that which has called me to the circle; and by this joining, once again I pledge myself to the Lady and the Faith. In her name, so shall it be. Thus the rite is done.'

The final act, though not part of the rite, is to set the staff up in the open at the full of the moon. Then, with the stang between you and the lunar disc, pour a cup of wine, using a short prayer of your own composing or, as I do, the Sangreal Prayer. Raise the cup on high, using your own or the Sangreal Prayer as a form of consecration:

Beloved Bloodmother of my especial breed,
Welcome me at this moment with your willing womb.
Let me learn to live in love with all you are,
So that my seeking spirit serves the Sangreal.

A few moments of silence, and then a small libation of wine is poured on the ground:

'To the Goddess in all her glory and beauty. Long may she inspire my thoughts and mind to her service.'

The second libation is poured at the foot of the staff, making sure that some of the wine splashes over the base of it. At the same time, the words used are:

'To Oak King, Ash King and Greenwood Lord. May some of the powers held by you be granted a residence within this your symbol.'

The rest of the wine is drunk as a toast, and just before drinking, the words used are:

'In honour of Our Lady and all those of our congregation. May some of the peace and understanding that I have found here be passed on to them, in the name of the fellowship and the coven. In her name, so be it done.'

Once again, I must stress that, from this moment on, the stang is no longer just an ash pole but a charged symbol of the craft, and as such should be used with respect.

2 The Coven Regalia

As mentioned before, certain vessels and articles are of a sacred nature within the craft. Now that a look has been taken at the knife and stang at a personal level, the next things to deal with are the coven tools. These are: the cup, the knife, the altar stangs, the besom, the sword and the cauldron. There are some covens that regard other articles – such as the shears and sieve – as part of the coven tools, but as these are peculiar to their tradition, they are best left out of this present work.

Of all the tools, the three most important are the cup, the knife, and the stang. With these three tools a group can start working the full rites, and add the other tools later. Of the other three, the order of precedence is the besom, the sword and the cauldron. One thing to remember is that any oath taken on the sword can be taken on the coven knife, used as a substitute for the sword. Even though a coven or group may not have all these articles, the meanings and attributes that they symbolize should be understood by the membership. Once again I must stress that these things are being dealt with at a basic level. Further research into these tools is certainly rewarding, and the knowledge gained is added to both coven and clan lore.

The Cup

This is one of the tools with a duality of meaning. On the one hand, it is representative of the female sex organs. On the other, it is representative of the Cauldron of Inspiration, the attribute of the ancient Druidic goddess Cerridwen. It is one of the pagan symbols which became

Christianized into the concept of the Holy Grail (see *The Mysteries of Britain* by Lewis Spence).

At the same time, in the dedication of the wine, it symbolizes both aspects together. By examining the dedication rites of the cakes and wine, it can be seen how this comes about. 'For by joining cup and knife we symbolize the joining of the two elements for the continuation of life. For this cup shall be the symbol of the Mother, and the knife the symbol of the Horned King.'

Apart from the recorded stories of virgin birth, human life needs both male and female elements for its creation. Even though people have been experiencing it for thousands of years, each and every birth is still a miracle in itself. We know the mechanics of conception, yet we cannot say what life is. Life can be reproduced in a laboratory, but it cannot be isolated as a substance so that one could say, 'This is N milligrams of life.' Life is the spark of divinity that animates the soul. By holding up the cup to the knife, we are hoping that the symbolic sexual act will charge the wine with the very essence or energy of that life force.

Even though it is symbolic, there are a few historical hints that certain strong priest-magicians were able to transmute the wine into another substance imbuing it with magical properties. The chance of our seeing this in our lifetime, or any other life for that matter, is very remote, but by performing the symbolic act, we live in hope (or perhaps better to say dread) that a spontaneous charging will occur. To partake of a truly charged cup could and would change us to the extent that our lives would never be the same again – that is, if there was a life left for us afterwards. To partake of the Godhead in such a way means that we must cease to be individuals and become as one and part of that Godhead. Thus the cup becomes the chalice of both love and fear, to be partaken of with reverence and dread.

'I call upon the Mother to charge this cup with the wisdom of the cauldron, that it may be passed on to us her followers.'

In this way, one prays that an external force will activate the inner knowledge that is locked up within everyone, making them more aware of what they are and where they sprang from; in other words, the roots from which they came.

On another level and in a magical sense, we are partaking of a ritual sacrificial feast. At the time of the sacrifice of the Divine King, some of the blood would be caught in a cup and mixed with some other drink. Sips of this would be drunk by the priesthood as a means of absorbing a portion of the sacrificed person's divinity. The rest of the blood would be sprinkled over the congregation as a blessing. Of course, time modified the concept, and gradually water would have come to be used in its place.

To charge the cup, the male symbol of the knife is inserted into the female symbol of the cup in imitation of the act of creation. Thus, by sympathetic magic, the wine is charged with a life force containing within it all the elements to be found in the Blood Royal – *Sang Real* – of the sacrifice. Christianized, it is the act of transubstantiation. To the coven, it is the charging of the wine with a divine life force or spirit.

At another level, the cup is the instrument of sharing. Just as everyone present at the meeting joins in the rites and shares a common practice and aim, so the sharing of the cup is symbolic of the sharing of the feast of the Goddess. Taken in her name and blessed by her, it means that some portion of her power is transferred, first into the wine and then to the congregation. By doing this, there is a joining of kindred minds in a common bond of fellowship, linking each individual member of the group to the other members of the coven.

As said before, the cup and the cauldron are interchangeable as a concept. Within this concept are found the Grail legends, a mystery within a mystery. The *Sangreal* or *Sang Real* is the Great Sacrament hidden within the body of the Christian Church, yet disapproved of by that Church partly because it is a blending of pre-Christian and Christian myths.

The occult significance of the Grail Cup is part of the craft mythos as well, and poses the question: 'Whom does the Grail serve?' or, 'Who makes the Wasteland bloom?' Within the answering of this question lies the heart of the Lady.

The Coven Knife

This is found mainly in established covens or groups. As the coven knife shares all the aspects of the personally owned knife, very often the knife owned by the Lord of the East is used to consecrate the cakes and wine.

In one sense, the coven knife is representative of the temple sacrificial knife, a blade which was used for no other purpose than the ritual killing of the sacrificial victim. Dedicated to the gods of a clan, tribe or later a city state, the knife would be used for the killing of the Divine King sacrificed on May Eve, and the dispatching of the sacred messenger to the gods. With the change from human to animal sacrificial victims, the knife as an instrument of death declined in use, being replaced by the pole-axe. Even then, the ritual knife was still to be found on the altars of the gods.

In the Capitoline Museum, Rome, is a well-preserved section of frieze from the Temple of Vespasian. Among the sacrificial implements shown are the pole-axe and the knife. The state faith of the Roman Empire placed great emphasis on the taking of the auspices from the liver of the sacrificial victim. In this case, the knife would be used to remove the liver and to prepare the sacred portions of the carcass for the altars of the gods.

Though the coven knife is no longer used in the faith as an instrument of blood sacrifice, it is still a blade that is dedicated to the service of the Goddess and as such has a place upon her altar. In this case, referring to the coven lucky enough to have an area that can be declared *territoria sacra*, where the coven regalia can be set up as an altar, care must be taken in selecting a place where this can be done.

Some people set this area up in a spare bedroom, which raises the question, 'How far up or down does a sacred place go? Is the room underneath part of that area as well?' As a Christian concept, the opinion was a definite 'Yes.' In the past, this led to an uncertainty in the use of monastic sub-vaulting, when this was incorporated into a more modern building used for a secular purpose. If the area was once under the high altar, was it part of the sacred area? So before setting up a permanent altar to the Goddess, some thought must be given as to where it should be and what is involved in setting it up. My own feeling about the matter is that the coven regalia should be held by the officers and brought by them to the meetings.

As the cup is the vessel of the Lady, so the coven knife is the instrument of the Officer of the East or his counterpart in the dedication of the cakes and wine. In his hands, as the knife of dedication of both elements of the feast, the knife is nothing more nor less than a phallic symbol. Once again, the joining-together of cup and knife is symbolic of the sexual act. Just as sexual intercourse can lead to the creation of life in the form of a child, so the symbolic coupling of the priest and the priestess through the union of cup and knife is the channel through which some of the power of the Goddess can flow, thus charging the cup with a life force or energy.

In most cases, this is purely a symbolic act, though one of deep significance and meaning, but on some occasions the symbol becomes reality. The wine and cakes are charged with the power of the Goddess. When this occurs, a subtle change comes over the rites. Instead of you working the rites, the ritual starts working you. From the moment the knife touches the wine, everything the group intends doing goes by the board. Instinctively, everyone knows what to do next and what is to follow. It is very similar to the action of the spark plugs of an engine – bang, bang, bang, and the power flows! The union between the Goddess and the congregation is a two-way flow of energy or force, set in an area of non-time. Everything in the circle seems to stand still for this period. There is a feeling of heightened awareness and emotion. Things are felt with a greater intensity and understanding. Somehow, for a few moments, time and place cease to exist. You then know what it means to be able to spin without motion between two worlds.

Even though everyone feels physically drained by this, a sense of euphoria seems to well up from deep inside. Every one of the senses seems to be in some way enhanced. Things take on a clarity and intensity that are not of this world. Knowledge and instinct become intertwined and as one. Everybody knows with certainty that they have seen and felt some part of the magic of the circle.

One is often left with an overwhelming feeling of sadness at the end of the ritual. Something gained for a few moments is then lost for ever; yet deep inside there is the knowing that what has been gained through the experience and involvement will later blossom into greater understanding. Thus, in Our Lady's own time and choosing, the pledge of both cup and wine is shared with us, her congregation.

One other use for the coven knife is that in some newly formed groups it can be – and very often is – substituted for the coven sword in the rite of oath-taking. In fact, some covens dispense with the sword altogether. Once again, this is a matter for the individuals of the group to decide on. When the knife does replace the sword, however, the one thing that it must never be used for is judgment or justice. In this case, one is 'called to the sword, and by the sword judged'. The coven knife as such can never fulfil this function.

On a more prosaic level, there has always been some question as to what shape the coven knife should be. Looking at it as a concept, the knife over the years has evolved to suit its function. From the first flint knife through the double-edged dagger to the curved, broad-bladed knife on the Roman altar, the sacred knife has taken on a shape suitable to its purpose. Today, as the use of it is purely one of ritual, the coven knife is usually of the double-edged and pointed variety.

By tradition, the knife should be hand-forged by a skilled member of the group. In most cases, however, the knife is bought and then dedicated to the faith. The one thing that must be remembered is that, like all tools of the faith, the knife has to be made ritually clean, consecrated and then dedicated to the Goddess. Unlike the personally owned knife, this is done in the presence of the whole coven or group, even though the actual rite of purification is done by the Lady and the Lord of the East in private. Then and only then is the knife ready to play its part within the coven rites.

The Coven Stangs

Once again it must be pointed out that, unlike the rest of the coven regalia, both stang and knife are to be found at two levels within a working group. The personal stang and knife share all the same attributes as the coven tools, the only difference being that the coven stang and knife take on a more formal role within the rites.

One other point to be noted is the use of the plural 'stangs' in the title. Traditionally, the ash stang is the staff of normal circle workings. On the very, very rare occasions on which the coven has to defend itself or one of its members against an attack from the outside, the blackthorn stang is brought into the circle.

As it is a wood of ill omen, the only use of the blackthorn stang is in the solemn rite of a formal cursing. In this guise, it is the representative of the Two-Faced God. From the same stem comes the power that can be used for both good and evil; a face which should be rarely invoked or worked. In twenty years of occult practice, I have been involved in only one formal cursing. Even though this cursing was thoroughly deserved, to say that the feelings engendered by this rite were most unpleasant could be classed as the understatement of the year. Yet, having said this, the formal cursing is a weapon in the armoury of the faith, but one that should rarely ever be used in defence of ourselves.

As stated before, the ash stang as a concept is representative of the God-King of the woodland glade; also of the reincarnated spirit of the Old King in the Young Horned God-Child of the Mother, in her aspect of Diana of the Greenwoods. In a coven sense, the ash stang is the guardian of the gateway of the circle, the link between the world of the Goddess and the world of the circle. One of its aspects is that of Herne the Hunter, as the god of hunting as well as fertility. In this guise he is the one who leads the Wild Hunt at Candlemas. Riding the Night Mare with the Hounds of Hell at his heels, he chases the souls of the dead into the underworld.

The vicinity of the Great Oak in Windsor Great Park is reputed to be haunted by the spectre of Herne around

Candlemas. The connection of Herne with the oak is found in the Oak-King, Ash-King and Greenwood Lord concepts. The mighty oak, guardian of the door, or the sacred ash, symbol of birth and rebirth, being set outside the circle, presides over the circle workings from his position in the north. By turning the staff round, it presides over the feast held after the rite. This repositioning of the stang in relation to the feasting group reaffirms the aspect of the Horned Child and the Mother, as represented by the Lady of the South. It is the son presiding over the feast in honour of the Goddess.

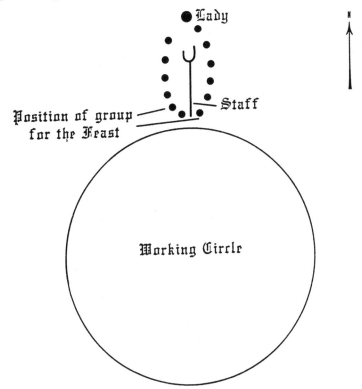

For all four major rites, the coven stang is dressed with arrows and garlands. Once again, the arrows are symbolic of the duality of the Horned God concept. They are a reminder of the concept of the god of the hunt; they are also a reminder that one of the many faces of the Goddess is that of the Divine Huntress. When tying the crossed arrows point upwards on the stang, we are reminding ourselves of these ancient concepts.

By stringing wire around the crossed arrows, the garland can be fixed to it. As for the make-up of the garland, this is dependent on the rite being worked.

Starting with the Candlemas ritual, the stang should be garlanded with yew twigs. As the tree of mourning, the yew is symbolic of the death of the old year. As Candlemas is in effect the start of the ritual year, the yew commemorates the final passing of the year that is gone. If there is any difficulty in getting hold of yew twigs, the stang is mounted with arrows but left ungarlanded. An ungarlanded stang is symbolic of the landscape at that time of year. The trees are bare and leafless, the fields empty. Yet if a close look is taken at nature, the signs of new life are there. So it is with the Candlemas ritual. The seed of inspiration is planted, the fire of life is rekindled.

At the May Eve rite, the stang should be garlanded with a mixture of birch, hazel, willow and hawthorn sprigs. Birch is considered to be feminine and lucky, as the tree of rebirth. Hazel is connected with fertility, fire, poetry, divination and knowledge. Finally, both hawthorn and willow are generally recognized as trees of ill luck and mourning; but on May Day sprigs of both are considered lucky, provided they are not brought into the house.

Lammas is of course a time of thanksgiving for all that the year has brought to the coven. So as this is the time of harvesting of the seed planted at Candlemas, the most appropriate garland for the stang comprises stalks of grain. The harvested grain is symbolic of the coven spirit and lore developed over the past months. The time gap between Lammas and Hallowe'en is the period of reflection, on what the past has meant to the individual as well as the lessons learnt within the group.

Hallowe'en is the time of the dead. As this rite differs from any of the others in the use of the twin circles, it must be remembered that the main part of the rite takes place in the second circle. If the stang is to be garlanded at all, it must be with yew. (For myself, I prefer just the crossed arrows, without a garland, for this ritual; but this is my own personal feeling. Once again, it is up to the individuals concerned to decide what they would like.) As this is the time of remembrance and mourning, as well as being symbolic of the crossing from one world to the other, the stang and the garland as such are not of the circle being worked.

One question that is always raised is, 'Why all these different things in the garland?' Quite simply, they are physical symbols of concepts within the faith, emblems to remind us of what we are working for at any particular rite. They are a little like the token ash faggot which is given at Yule for good luck and then burned at the following Yule. (These symbols are a minute part of a very complex language and lore of the trees. This is a subject worthy of study in greater detail, certainly not one for inclusion in this present work because of its sheer complexity, but an introduction to it is given in the Appendix.) Again, it should be made clear that the use of these woods etc is not mandatory. After all, it is not everyone who can get hold of them. If you can get them, by all means do so; but if you cannot get them, other greenery will serve just as well. It is the concept that is important, not the symbols.

The blackthorn being an ominous tree, when used as a stang it stands for the dark side of the craft. In some ways it represents the two-faced head: one face is the face of good, and one the face of evil. The power is neutral. It is the end it is used for that is important. In the case of the blackthorn stang as an altar, the use of the power raised is to harm. Once again, it must be stressed that this is something not to be undertaken lightly. The only time this is ever done is when there is nothing else left that can be used in its place.

For instance, if someone keeps parking in front of your driveway, it is far better to thump them than to curse them. By using the rite of cursing, the group involved can and very often does find that a whole year's work is lost. The feelings and emotions surfacing during the cursing can upset the group atmosphere for quite a while. People tend to avoid each other. They no longer open themselves up at meetings. Once the dark side of people has been brought to the fore, it is a difficult job to suppress it again.

So why include the act of cursing in the first place? Just as life is not all sweetness and light, neither is the faith. The ability to take a magical revenge on the enemies of the coven is an intrinsic part of the craft; and the whys and whens of this power should be understood by anyone practising the rites. The other thing to be noted is that, for a rite of cursing, the stang is never garlanded.

Because of the dangers inherent in the cursing ritual, the actual working of the rite has been left out. This rite is known to all groups within the clan, and there it will stay. Publishing it could lead to the temptation to use it, while only half understanding the moral issues involved when deciding to work it. In twenty-odd years, I have had recourse to this rite only once; and I feel that having to do it again in the next twenty years would be too soon. Anyone wishing to include a formal cursing rite in their workings must find their own path. Only by exploring the concepts and mechanics of a formal cursing can all the dangers inherent in the working of this type of rite be fully understood.

In the creating of a coven stang, because of the more formal and ceremonial aspects involved, the make-up of the stang is different from that of the personal stang. The individual's stang is very often just a forked ash staff. The coven stang is by tradition an ash staff mounted by a pitchfork head or a socketed pair of iron 'horns'. Dependent on the guardian animal totem spirit adopted by the group, coven or clan, so a mask of that animal will be fixed at the base of the two prongs. This creates a symbol of the young Horned God in the aspect of the coven guardian spirit. Primitive, maybe, but as an identification mark, straight away it acts as a key to all the concepts involved in the clan workings.

The ram's head mask mounted below the prongs of our coven staff needs no explaining. Everyone in the clan knows what it means and what it stands for. The same can be said for the blackthorn stang. The small stag mask mounted beneath the prongs is the key to the concept of Herne the Hunter and his hounds, the concept involved in a cursing.

By the placing of the animal mask on the stang, we are reaching back into prehistory, and the animal guardian spirit or totem of the group. By saying, for instance, 'I'm of the clan of the Roebuck' means a more personal involvement with your coven or group than just saying, 'I'm a member of a coven.' In this way the spirit of the coven can be enhanced and enlarged to form the spirit of the clan.

Shodding with Iron

As noted before, both the personal and the coven stang should be shod with iron after the rite of consecration. Behind this action is a long history of magical theory. The connection of smithcraft and magic stems from the little-understood and therefore magical way in which apparent stones could be treated with fire to yield up iron. By a further use of fire, this substance could be shaped and formed into all sorts of things. Within the person of the smith were found the skills and knowledge to do this. Like most trade secrets, they were purported to be of divine origin, and were revealed only to the select few after a long period of service with a master – a sort of ancient 'closed shop'.

In theory, the unnatural iron was able to neutralize the natural magic of a spell. From this train of thought arose the idea that a witch could not cross iron. Like a battery, the stang is charged with a magical power at the consecration. Because that power cannot cross iron, by shodding the staff with iron, the power was unable to run to earth and remained within the body of the stang. So by fixing the nail into the bottom of the stang at its consecration, you are in effect containing within the body of the staff the magical power of the Goddess, thus making it a truly charged altar of her creation.

The Besom

In spite of all the illustrations that show a female witch riding on her broomstick, the broom or besom as such is, and always has been, a male tool. When a female witch 'rode the besom', it was certainly not in the way shown in most books; rather something of a more basic nature. The component parts of the besom are both male and female. As such, they are purely sexual in symbology and interpretation.

No one can be quite sure as to when the besom became an accepted part of the tools of the craft. There are hints of its use from medieval witch trials. There are also hints of the use of an artificial penis or dildo. The rites of those days relied heavily on sex magic. The Devil or Magister of the coven would be expected to serve at least three or four women at one meeting. Hence one of the things which came out in the old witch trials was the story that when a woman had intercourse with 'the Devil', his penis was always cold and hard and even quite painful for the woman concerned. Without delving too deeply into matters of sex magic at this stage, it is easy to see how one end of the besom came to be carved into the shape of a penis. It represented the cold, hard member of the Devil himself. Following this tradition, the handle of the besom is still shaped in this way at one end.

The actual brush part of the besom is the female

The Besom

component and is made up of certain twigs. Once again, these twigs are part of the language and lore of the trees. Like the garland on the stang, they say and mean something to the initiated. The first kind of twig to be found in the besom is of course the birch, the tree of birth and rebirth. Then there is the hazel, which is the tree of fire, fertility, poetry, divination and knowledge. Finally comes the yew, the tree of death and resurrection. Looking at these woods, the message is quite simple. Only through birth will there be life. From that life will come poetry, art and knowledge. Yet because of birth, there must be death, and with death, rebirth or resurrection. But only by the joining of the male and female can birth and life be achieved. By the joining of the handle to the brush, the symbolic act of creation is performed.

The besom's place within the rites is that of the bridge between the world of the circle and the world outside. Being a male tool, it is always in the care of East, or whoever is casting the circle. Placed between the two markers in the north, and across the perimeter of the circle, everyone entering the sacred ring must cross it from left to right. The brush end, being representative of the vagina or womb, is always placed inside the circle.

When everyone has been helped into the circle by the Lady, she closes it by bringing the besom inside the perimeter. Where the coven or group have decided that the cakes, the wine-cup and the wine will be left at the foot of the stang until needed, the Lady will have to leave the circle to collect them. In order to do this, she replaces the besom across the perimeter of the circle as before, and crosses it from right to left. Carrying the cakes, wine-cup and wine, she then re-enters the circle by crossing the besom from left to right. Then she re-closes the circle by bringing the besom back into the ring after her.

When the rite is finished, again everyone leaves the circle by crossing the besom, from right to left. The Lady being the last one to leave, she closes the circle again by taking the besom out of it. East then reverses the face of the stang for the feast.

The symbology involved within the using of the besom as a bridge once again refers to and reinforces the concept of the Goddess as the Mother figure. Within the womb of the Mother, we are protected from the outside. In another sense, we are entering the womb-cave of the cauldron. By working in the circle, we begin to understand something of the complex relationship between humanity and divinity, as well as the inter-relationship between humanity and our environment found within the forces of nature. Anything humans can do, nature can undo. By destroying nature's balance, we destroy ourselves. The whole of humanity is as much a servant of nature as any other form of life within its spectrum.

Today, science and mysticism are regarded as separate things. Yet in the past, both were an indivisible part of the concept of divine harmony and balance. In the two elements of the besom are the opposites of male and female. Bring the two together, and you have balance and harmony summed up in the word love.

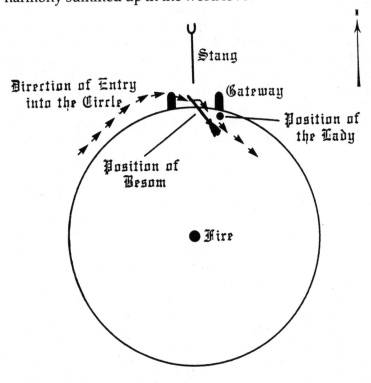

So when the besom is laid across the threshold of the circle, it symbolizes an expression of hopes within a prayer, as well as certain basic truths. As both handle and brush are joined, so we by the sexual act were given life. Within the unborn child lie the seeds of all the things which make a human being a thinking person. In the twigs of birch, hazel and yew, we see the symbols of being born, the faculties of being able to think, reason, understand, hate, love, create and dream. Then as birch is to life, so yew is to death. Through being born, the body we have now must one day die. By placing the besom across the threshold of the circle, we are acknowledging the fact that there is a world other than the one we are in now. Also, that there are two parts to our being, the body and the soul. The body belongs to this world, the soul comes from that which is of the other world. United they form the life-form or body that is ourself today. By crossing the broom, we are crossing over into the world of mysticism and the spirit.

From that crossing, we hope to bring back a measure of understanding: the understanding of why we were born, the feelings, thoughts and emotions that help to make us what we are; the motive that drives us to search for ourselves and our kindred souls. Through involvement in the circle workings, we come to accept the restless driving urge that the Fates have placed upon us to seek answers to the mystery that is inherent in life. We come to accept this destiny with understanding, so that when it is time for the divine spark that is in all of us to return to its place of origin, we can say in all truth, 'I have learnt. Now let me rest a while.'

One other aspect of the besom's being placed across the circle that should not be forgotten is the healing of the spirit. Many of us who follow the Way of the Goddess start off by being lost in our own time. We are displaced within the framework of our society, out of step and understanding with our own age. We are like a wounded person blundering around in a dark and threatening wood. Lost, lonely and afraid, we come across a clearing, and in this glade is a mature and beautiful woman. She soothes the hurt and cleans and binds our wounds, gives us comfort, peace and, above all, understanding. When we leave this glade, we know that we will be able to find our way back to this secret haven and that the Goddess will be there to tend our wounds again. Within her circle we can re-find ourselves; in her sanctuary, heal the spirit and find a peace of mind beyond all understanding. Thus her circle can be all things to all people, and the besom the bridge between the two.

Once again it must be stressed, as in the case of the coven cup, knife and stang, that only the basic attributes of these things have been given here. Also, at this stage it must be remembered that much of the coven regalia will be found only in long-established groups. The absence of any of these tools in no way affects the validity of the rites. You simply adapt to what you have and leave the rest in the hands of the Goddess. In her own time, she will give you what she thinks you need.

The Coven Sword

Historically speaking, the inclusion of the sword in the coven regalia is not all that old. The sword, being one of the marks of a gentleman, would have been out of place in the hands of a coven member as for years the practising members of a coven would be the old 'wise-woman' or the 'cunning-man' of the village. Because of the dangers of being thought in any way heretical, the full group would meet up only at night, a few times in a year. For a peasant to be seen with a sword in his possession would certainly lead to questions being asked; not something a member of the old faith would look forward to.

This is not to say that there were no landowners within the ranks of the faith. I am quite sure there were. On financial grounds alone, they would certainly be the leaders. Also, they would be the ones to have the unquestionable freedom of movement denied to the peasant classes. Moreover, being responsible for the appointment of the parish priest and the payment of any patronage attached to the church, they could quietly advise any priest to keep his nose out of the lord of the manor's business and to leave certain people alone – or else!

Another case where being leader of a group would certainly be of advantage to any landowner would be in the handling of his livestock and the customary service rendered for the land and cot holdings of the peasant cultivator. In the age of superstition, anyone harming that person's cattle or crops could find themselves on the end of a cursing, arranged by the landowner in the form of the masked coven leader. Placing certain people under the protection of the Goddess would mean that such an order became more in the nature of a divine command, to be passed around by the local wise-woman or witch. Being local to the scene, she would be the one who would know the persons likely to harm livestock out of spite or revenge. In this way certain groups would list the sword among the coven tools, because the leader, being a man of wealth and property, would not be seen without one.

Today the sword is more common and has become one of the accepted things. In this light, I can only say how we use the sword and what it stands for within our workings. For us, the sword is an instrument of oath-taking. Also, it is a symbol of justice and judgment when dealing with an act of banishment or formal cursing.

Apart from the rite of justice, banishment and cursing, there is no other function of the sword that cannot be fulfilled by the knife, making the sword something that is usually found in established covens or groups. For the ceremony of oath-taking, the sword would be used as directed in the oath of membership, the oath of office and the oath of the Lady. When used for justice, the person is called to the sword, and by the sword judged.

This act in itself is not a magical ritual and would normally be held in an unconsecrated circle, with the members forming up around the edge of it. Whether or not the person accused of causing the harm is there, the person making the claim must state, while holding the blade of the sword, that what they are saying is true. If the person accused is present, they must do the same while refuting the allegations. Anyone else who has anything to say on the matter may say it on oath and by the sword. Should a decision be made to banish a member formally, for harming the coven or group or other members, this will be done at a specially called meeting and will be performed within a consecrated circle and the sentence pronounced by the Lady. It is then the duty of East, as the keeper of records, to inform all other groups within the clan of what has been done.

A member who feels that there is good cause for it is entitled to ask for a formal cursing as well as support for this cursing from every member of the clan. The first step is to bring the matter before East or the Lady, if they feel there are grounds for some sort of revenge to be taken against some outsider or a banished member of the coven or clan. Then an informal meeting of the membership is called and the matter put before them.

Once again, this meeting is held in an unconsecrated circle, and the person desiring the cursing must swear by the sword that they are giving a true account of the facts. On top of this, the person must pledge that they will abide by the verdict of the majority decision if the request is turned down. As stated before, a formal cursing is not something to be undertaken lightly, because of the effect it can have on a group. But if it is decided that a cursing is warranted, the next thing to be decided is if it will involve the other groups within the clan, or whether it will be done at coven level. A date will be set, usually during the dark of the moon, when it will be done.

If the other covens of the clan are to be involved in this rite, East will inform them of the reasons, intent, time and place, and the name of the person or persons involved. Naturally, the rite will be held in a consecrated circle, and the Lady will use the sword to pronounce the formal curse and direct it at the person or persons who have now become the common enemy of the clan. Once again, it must be stressed that a formal cursing is not something that is hurled at all and sundry on the spur of the moment. It is a final weapon in our armoury for defending ourselves or our fellow members against the outside world. As such, it is used only rarely and with very, very great care. Remember, curses can and sometimes do rebound.

Like the knife, the sword should be hand-forged by a member of the coven. But once again, how many people have the skills to do this? So in the case of most groups or covens, the swords are bought – and very expensive they can be, too. In the group I was first associated with, the coven sword was an old shortsword picked up in a junk shop, with the hilt refurbished by the Magister. In the same way, I picked up an old sword-blade, and he as an ex-smith offered to rebuild the hilt for me. This was going to be all metal, file-worked into a castle-and-rose design. The crossguard was going to be the same as the coven sword, with a downward-pointing 'Hand of Glory'. I had made the crossguard, and the castle-and-rose hilt was almost finished, when he died. My sword, along with his, disappeared – a loss I have never ceased to bewail. But returning to the question of swords, if an old blade can be obtained, the hilt can be refashioned to suit the ideas the coven feel belongs to the sword.

In the case of the downturned 'Hand of Glory' on the guard of the sword, the symbology behind this is obvious. The pointing finger is warding off evil or directing the power raised in a magical rite in the circle. In this case, the sword replaces the magician's wand as the instrument for directing that power – for instance, in the case of directing a curse.

The castle-and-rose design that was intended for my sword hilt can still be seen painted on the cabins and furniture of some traditional river barges. There is a claim that the castle and rose refer to Windsor Castle and the English rose of royalty. Maybe; but at the same time the symbols of the castle and rose should be looked at in the context of the Glass Castle of Welsh mythology, or the castle that spins without motion between two worlds, while the rose is 'the Rose beyond the Grave', the first bloom from the wasteland restored to its vigour. Once again, this is part of the death-and-resurrection cycle of the Goddess.

There is no strictly traditional wood that should be used in the hafting of the sword. So whatever wood is used is a matter of personal preference. For myself, I like to have elder. In the list of sacred woods, the elder tree is not only considered unlucky but also a tree that is associated with witchcraft. One other aspect of the elder is that it was often regarded as feminine, and often a seat of judgment was set up under it.

There is an old and long-established way of dealing with the taking of elder; but the main thing is, it should be left for a year to dry. When this is done, strip the bark from it, cut and shape it into a handgrip and then fix it to the sword. The one trouble with elder is that it tends to crack and splinter, so care must be taken to make sure that it is sanded down well. The only other thing that has to be thought about is that, like all coven tools, it has to be cleansed and dedicated to the faith. The rites for doing this will be dealt with elsewhere in the book.

The Cauldron

It should be borne in mind that, even though the cauldron and the cup have many attributes common to each other, the symbolic significance of the cauldron goes far beyond that of the cup. One could say that time itself, instead of enriching the mythos of the cauldron, has stripped much of it away. The coven cauldron at one time was the famed cauldron of Cerridwen, the Undry or the cauldron from which each in proportion to their station and merit were fed. It was the cauldron of Bran which gave life to the dead. It was the cauldron in which magical potions and brews were prepared. Finally, in a coven sense, it is also the cauldron of divination. Partly filled with water, and with something shiny in the bottom of it to act as a focal point of concentration, it is used as a magical mirror for seeing into the future. In the hands of a practised diviner, this can be a useful magical tool.

Ritually, the coven cauldron is symbolic of the Cauldron of Inspiration found in the castle of Celtic myth. Traditionally guarded by nine maidens, this is the cauldron of the Pale-Faced Goddess. Within the cauldron are contained all knowledge and inspiration. To drink from it is to gain that knowledge and understanding.

Yet, at the same time, this is the cauldron of life. As with the cauldron of the Celtic god Bran, it restores life to the dead. Thus as life comes from the cauldron, so must all the things that are of life come from the cauldron, too – love, hate, courage, cowardice, greed, generosity, bigotry, understanding, birth, death and rebirth; in short, all the things which make people what they are. (I am not the only one to interpret the symbolism of the cauldron in this way. In that strange old book *The Rosicrucians: Their Rites and Mysteries*, first published in 1870, its author Hargrave Jennings says: 'We claim the cauldron of the witches as, in the original, the vase or urn of the fiery transmigration, in which all the things of the world change.')

By going to the cauldron of the Goddess in the form of working her rites, you begin to understand something of yourself, to recognize the shortcomings in your own make-up. With this understanding comes the knowledge that things can be changed by an act of will. This is part of the creed, in the words 'So shall it be.' Perhaps it would be better to say, 'So shall it be, because I will it so', because with involvement comes understanding, and with understanding comes change.

The more one involves oneself in the ways of the Goddess, the more one becomes aware of 'I' – not 'I' as a solitary entity but 'I' as a part of this living planet; part of the ebb and flow of time, space and nature, being able to see the harmony and balance of life and nature and become as one with that harmony and balance. To use the gifts of the Goddess wisely, because they are ours only for this lifetime on the understanding that, when taking something, something must be put back. The devotion to her worship is taken by the Goddess, to be replaced by understanding from her cauldron.

A mark of this understanding of what the cauldron stands for is found in the May Eve rites. Before starting the feast after the ritual, East draws the attention of the Lady to the cauldron at the foot of the stang, with the words: 'What of the potion at the foot of the altar, Lady?' Her reply is: 'A reminder to us all that within the milk of the Mother is the sweetness of life mingled with the bitterness of disappointment. Thus a balance is struck. For the goodness on one hand is countered by the sorrow on the other. For by placing them at the foot of the altar within the cauldron, we accept this from the gods and draw a measure of wisdom from it.'

To find the Holy Grail, the knight had to be perfect: honourable, chaste, charitable and brave; in short, to possess all the virtues which distinguished the knight from the commoner. In the Mysteries of the Cauldron, the seeker after the truth of the sacred vessel must in turn possess certain virtues. To find the blessing of the Cauldron-Grail, one must seek first with understanding. Understanding, that is, of the nature of the quest – is one doing it through a basic desire to learn for the love of knowledge and understanding? Or is one seeking to gain power for self-aggrandizement?

By the understanding of self, the unfolding magic of the cauldron can begin. To seek within this understanding the very nature of divinity and the personal relationship between divinity and man. To see that within every living thing there is a small spark of that divinity and, on a personal level, to allow that divinity to blossom from within and grow stronger. Eventually, the wisdom gained through this blossoming, your relationship with others and your own life, is one of involvement, understanding and compassion.

This is not to say that you must live a life of 'turning the other cheek'. Far from it. You must try to understand why certain people do certain things. You must understand your own motives for rejecting or stopping that person if they act in a certain way towards you. When acting against them, you must ask yourself the reasons for doing so. Is it a question of 'I want, so I think I must', instead of saying 'I feel that this must be done' and accepting the responsibility for it?

In retrospect, the usage of the cauldron in the rites is shrouded in the mists of time. Many and varied are the attributes and meanings that now surround it. In the Grail concept, certain parts of the cauldron mythos have been Christianized, while certain of the Christian elements have attached themselves to the cauldron. Due to the inherent multiplicity of symbolism connected with the vessel, these adaptations will fit very well into the overall concept. Thus when it is said that the Cauldron-Grail can be all things to all men, never a truer word was spoken. The thing that any group or coven must decide is what will the cauldron mean to them? What will it symbolize in the rites?

On a personal level, a cauldron can be and very often is used as an instrument of scrying, a means of inducing clairvoyance. In some cases, it is just one of those 'witchy' things that people like to have around them. In a coven sense, if the cauldron is to play a part in the rites, there must be a fully understood mythos and symbology attached to its usage. This means that many of the present known meanings of the cauldron must be looked at and some of them rejected because they do not fit in with what the cauldron will stand for within the group or coven rites. To be able to say, 'What the cauldron means to us is ...' is far better than saying, 'The cauldron means so-and-so and stands for such-and-such' and then trying to relate all these aspects to your own particular cauldron mythos. In this way, you can introduce a clarity and continuity into the symbolism of the cauldron, rather than trying to make sense of the multiplicity of present cauldron aspects and symbology, which can tend to become a mish-mash.

To me, the symbol of the cauldron is that of the vessel containing the medium of generation of ideas and thoughts. These ideas and thoughts are formless and expressionless; yet at the same time, they are potent with knowledge, which somehow has to be gained and earned. The cauldron in a mystical sense is the pool of existence in suspension. By this I mean that it is full of life past and life to come, the symbol of birth and rebirth. In death we return to this pool and await the coming rebirth. With rebirth come all the things which make up life – the triumphs, the sorrows, the joys and the sadness, the gifts of life and the payments we have to make for our past lives; one more step that we take on the spiral of spiritual awareness.

On another level, the cauldron is the vessel of inspiration, the place in which all will find their needs answered. In this sense, the cauldron is the cauldron of the mind. Within the self is the answer to many of the problems people set themselves. To explore oneself and one's motives is perhaps one of the hardest things to do. To subject oneself to a critical analysis, to try to explain one's motives for certain acts, is to gain insight and the ability to create change. Also there is the growing awareness of one's relationship to others, and the acceptance of the views of others even if they go against one's own train of thought. One lesson of the cauldron must be tolerance; another, understanding; thirdly, the ability to examine one's own ideas and thoughts in a constructive but critical way. When one goes to the Goddess with an open mind and heart, she will grant a portion of the wisdom of her cauldron.

Unlike the rest of the coven tools, the cauldron is one of the things that should be looked at as more a spiritual concept than a physical object. The actual vessel itself is nothing more than a trigger for the mystical concept of the cauldron. By placing it at the foot of the altar stang, it should create within the mind certain images and thoughts. Some groups when working indoors use a cast-iron cauldron for making a brew of punch, to which everyone present has contributed something. As a matter of pure symbolism, this is a good idea. Anything that can be used physically as an expression of a mystical concept can do nothing but good in helping to create the right frame of mind when working.

One thing to be remembered about the cauldron is that, as part of the coven regalia, its use within the rites is very limited. Many groups manage quite well without one. If anyone has a small cauldron that they wish to use, by all means let them do so. For myself, the concept of the cauldron and its meanings is far more important than the actual article itself. So each group should decide just what the significance of the cauldron will be to them.

The Skull

The skull is one of the articles which has long and well-known associations with many forms of occult thought and working. Yet in witch traditions it is not all that common an article; mainly, I suspect, because of the association of the skull with grave-robbery and dese-cration, Satanism, voodoo and so on. Perhaps the use of a skull in rituals came to be thought of as something evil, because of Christian thinking on the whole nature of any form of magical practice, as being against the word of God and being related to the Devil and the dark side of human nature.

At the same time, within the Christian Church there was and still is a recognition that the mortal remains of certain people – that is, the saints – possess certain powers. These powers were usually those of healing, and consequently such remains were treated as revered relics. Enshrined in splendid tombs, they became the focal-points of pilgrimages by the faithful. Such relics, accompanied by prayer, were believed to form a link with the spirit of the saint, in the hope of the faithfuls' being granted some request in the form of a miracle. In the same way, the skull within the witch rites acted as a focal point for a spirit to home in on; only this contact through the skull would be of a more personal nature to the group or coven, and confined to that group only.

In the past, many cultures have created a mythology of the skull or bones as cult objects. In the case of European thought, historically speaking, basically such ideas stem from the Celtic cult of the severed head. To the Celts, the head was the source of the spiritual power and life force of a man. By taking his head, the power of the dead man would be transferred to his killer and work in the latter's favour. By the holding of the head, the courage and bravery of the dead warrior could be called upon to act as a defence against any form of supernatural danger.

By decorating a house, stockade, gateposts or temple portals with skulls or severed heads of either the clan's enemies or those of the tribe, what was being stated was that this place or area was defended by the chained souls of the dead warriors. Believing that there is a relationship between the soul of the dead person and the head, very often the skull of a long-dead priest or shaman would be used as the focal-point in the ritual for the calling-back of the soul of the dead man from the other world. Because in life it was recognized to be the dwelling-place of the spiritual power of that living person, in death it became the now empty home of that same spirit. By ritual, that spirit could be recalled to that recognizable object to help and protect the now living members of the dead person's family, group or clan.

One of the things that we find difficult to realize today is that death was not the barrier between the two worlds that it is now. With the words 'Rest in peace', what we are saying or asking is that the soul of the dead person should stay in their world and not cross over into ours. Yet to the Celts, the worlds of the physical and the psychic intertwined on this plane. Instead of a clear-cut daylight or dark, there was a twilight realm through which certain people could cross the divide between the worlds of the living and the dead, bringing back information, while the dead could contact the living with the same aim in mind. In this way, the past and the future could be brought into the present. By recognizing this, it was considered possible for the soul to cross from the other world to this, the material world, in the form of a guardian and prophetic shade.

Because of the recognition of good being able to reach back from beyond the grave, it must stand to reason that evil could do the same. So supernatural protection against supernatural evil would be recognized as being needed. Thus the cult of the skull would grow to match the spiritual needs of any given age.

I suppose in many ways we have grown away from these concepts and ideas, and tend to regard them as a form of primitive fantasy and superstition. But just because we have done this, it does not mean that there is not more than a grain of truth behind them. Many people believe in the immortal soul; yet at the same time they deny the existence of ghosts. That the 'ghost' is an echo of a past event is just one of the theories doing the rounds at the present time. This ignores the recognition that, if there is an immortal soul within a person, that soul should have the power to return to a certain place that has some relevance from a past life.

In this sense, the skull within the circle is a recognition of this fact by certain groups. Moreover, the rites and rituals connected with the skull are in no way an attempt to call up the dead by incantation or to bind that soul or spirit into the service of the group. Any contact made from the other side will be on the basis of a willing and mutual acceptance of each other's world, in the context of just another witchcraft rite or practice.

One other word of warning. The fact that there is a use for a skull in certain aspects of craft practice is not a licence or reason for grave-desecration in the name of the faith. Groups can and do manage quite well without using a skull. In fact, some groups would never dream of bringing one into the circle. On this score, if a skull is obtained legally, perhaps from an antique shop or a supplier of medical schools, and the group as a whole feel the urge to use one, by all means do so. But remember, any group using a skull leaves itself open to all sorts of charges that would be difficult to refute.

One of the first actions that must be undertaken is the ritual cleansing of the skull. This is done with and in the name of the four elements of earth, air, fire and water. Behind this act is the recognition that the skull must be cleansed of all past connections. In an occult sense, the skull is not being used as a means of calling back the soul of the past owner, but rather as a means of attracting a shade of a past person with witch connections. In this sense, the skull acts as a key to recognition that, on the one hand, a group is working within a recognizable framework of 'The skull within the rites'. On the other hand, the members of the group are opening themselves up to a contact from across the river of oblivion.

On this score, there is the question of what exactly is contacted or comes through. Is it a person long dead and awaiting rebirth or an aspect of the old Horned God manifesting itself as a person? This is another one of those unanswerable questions. For myself, I think that in most cases it is a shade, spirit or soul of a person who has died within the faith. My reason for believing this is that, in the cases I have known in which a skull was being used, the contact gradually built up in a recognizable individual way. In one case, the contact was female, with a name and a clearly identifiable past life. In another instance (and in this I can only repeat what I have been told), the contact was male and rather fond of women and dirty jokes. Yet in both cases the contact became real and there was a flow of inspirational working material from these contacts through working with the individual skulls.

For the initial introduction of the skull into the circle, an indoor working is perhaps the best idea. Because of the passive nature of the rite, and the introduction with no actual movement being required, simplicity and patience are the keynotes. In the place of the flame in the centre of the circle, the skull is positioned between two candles, with all present sitting round it and facing inwards. This is where the patience comes in. In this case, it is just a matter of waiting for the first faint feeling of mutual contact. Gradually this will strengthen and build up, until a recognizable form and sex come through.

There is a certain amount of talk between the members of the group, as the impressions they feel concerning the identity of the contact emanating from the skull build-up. In the end, a mutually agreed name is found. The skull is then formally given that name and, by this naming, brought into the coven or group as one of the invisible members, part of the hidden company.

From the naming onwards, the persona of the contact tends to grow stronger and develop into a recognizable character with their own particular quirks and foibles. In this light, when the cup has been dedicated at any meeting, the practice is to pour a libation in their honour and memory; and rightly so, because of the call of like unto like. They too are part of the working group.

As a matter of interest, some three or four months before the break-up of my old group, there was a gradual feeling that our spirit contact was disengaging itself from the group. In the end, instinctively we knew that our skull was 'empty' and that our contact was staying firmly on the other side.

To some, all this will seem rather fanciful and a prime example of occult 'line-shooting'. To be frank, in the first instance I had my doubts as well. I had developed a sort of 'Oh, yeah? Well, I'm going to wait and see' attitude. But within a short time I felt that there was more to it than I had thought. There was a definite response through the skull. Surprisingly enough, it was not the sort of response I had expected. There was no sudden flow of esoteric knowledge, from what can only be described as a past leader contacting a new following on this side of the grave. It was more subtle than that, and infinitely more difficult to grasp.

It seemed to be an echo of a past life, with the echo of another past life. There was a sense of bafflement as to why she felt the call to our gathering. Gradually, as more and more of her nature became known to us, we realized that her shade or spirit was locked into her then present life. She was, as she had died in that life, not a follower of the Goddess. Having said this, underneath that particular memory there was another, and it was this past-life memory that was responding, through the last rebirth and death memory, and answering our call.

On some occasions, there was a distinct feeling of her not wanting to be there and a lack of understanding as to why she was there. On other occasions, there was the feeling of her willingness to be there and an understanding of what we were aiming at and trying to achieve. At these times, there was a feeling of our being linked to the past and reliving the past, which was reflected in the way the whole nature of the rites would change. At least two or three of us at the meeting would feel this more strongly than the others. At another time, it would be two or three of the others who would feel it; and within the ebb and flow of this contact, each of us came back with a greater understanding that had to be pondered over before being put to good use.

THE RITE OF PURIFICATION AND ACCEPTANCE

As stated before, in the first instance the skull must be ritually cleansed of all past influences. Should a skull be brought into a working circle before this is done, there is more than a good chance of its reactivating traumatic events from the past life, while at the same time throwing open the doors to other sorts of nastiness. Because of the unrealized nature of past events that emanate from the skull, the forces of chaos can and often do batten on and use the opening created by the skull to flood through. Once chaos has entered the circle, it takes a strong magical act to return it to its proper place. So on no account must an impure skull be brought into the circle.

As to the location and timing of this rite, in effect this is a matter for the group to decide. In the case of my own thinking, and because of the nature of the rite, I prefer the dark-of-the-moon period and making it a special event rather than slotting it in during a meeting. But, as I said before, this is a personal choice. Because of the need for a fairly large fire, rather than the token flame of a candle as used for inside working, the proper place is in a fully charged and consecrated circle outdoors. Once again, this is done with and in the name of the four elements of earth, air, fire and water. Four members must be chosen to play the parts of these elements and represent them in the correct ritual order.

Stage 1
If other members are going to be there during the rite, they should enter the circle first and gather round the edge just inside it. Then the four people representing the four elements enter. The person representing air places the skull by the fire, and the circle is then closed. With the four people representing the four elements standing still in the centre of the circle, the rest of the gathering start 'treading the mill' widdershins, until Air feels it is time to stop. Air then takes the skull in their right hand and uses the left hand as though they were physically drawing something down from the skull and out through the nostrils, at the same time using the words:
Air: 'As I draw the breath from thy nostrils ... so shall life and the memory of past life be drawn from thee.'

This is done three times, using the same words. Then the skull is put back by the fire. Earth comes forward and, standing close to the skull, says:
Earth: 'Lo ... I represent the Mother from whose womb all life must come ... also the place that with death all must return to ... and with the sprinkling of this earth ... I symbolize that return.'

This is once again said three times, and each time a little of the earth which has been carried into the circle for this purpose is sprinkled on the skull. Fire then takes the skull in their right hand and passes it through the flames with the left hand, using these words:

Fire: 'Thus from the grave and through the fires of purification thou shalt pass ... The place where both past and present are burned out from within thee.'

This is done three times, and the skull is then placed back by the fire. Water comes forward, using the words:

Water: 'With the waters of time and forgetfulness ... I wash away both past and present ... until such time as rebirth sends thee once again back into this world to live another life.'

Once again this is done three times, and each time a little water from the cup is sprinkled on the skull. With that, this part of the rite is finished.

Stage 2

The next stage, of course, is the naming. It should be made clear that, even if it is part of the rite of purification, this stage can be and often is done at a later date and usually outdoors. As mentioned before, the skull is brought into the circle, which has been cast for the occasion in the usual way. It should preferably be carried by a male member of the group. It is placed between two candles. The rest of the gathering then sit around it and link hands, while focusing attention on the skull. Gradually impressions begin to seep through, and if anyone gets a definite and strong impression, they should mention it. As the feeling builds up, a name, a past life-style and a general feeling about the contact come through. At some point, when it feels right, the officiating Lady takes the skull in her right hand and breathes into the nostril cavity, using these words:

Lady: 'Through Our Lady, for her, and in her name ... I breathe life from the group into thee ... In her name ... so be it done.'

She then puts the skull down and in the following order places three strands of coloured wool over the top of the skull, crossing each other:

First, the red strand, symbolic of the red cord of life through birth.

Second, the black cord of knowledge and token of full membership of the coven.

𝔗𝔬𝔭 𝔬𝔣 𝔱𝔥𝔢 𝔖𝔨𝔲𝔩𝔩 𝔴𝔦𝔱𝔥 𝔱𝔥𝔢 𝔱𝔥𝔯𝔢𝔢 𝔠𝔬𝔯𝔡𝔰 𝔦𝔫 𝔭𝔬𝔰𝔦𝔱𝔦𝔬𝔫

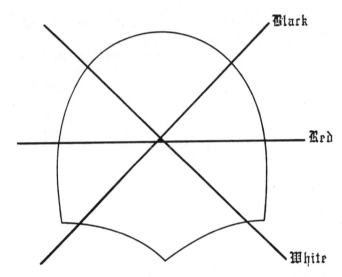

Third, the white cord of death and the world beyond
death.

At this stage, there should be a generally felt reaction. If
it feels good, that signifies acceptance. A little of the wine
that has been saved from the consecration is sprinkled
over the skull by the Lady, using these words:

Lady: 'In the name of [group, coven or clan name] and
with this wine ... I name thee [name], in the knowledge
that through this skull ... you choose to be called to us and
willingly join us to aid in our worship of the Old Gods ...
and, above all, the Goddess.'

Before the rite is closed, everyone shares a cup of wine
in honour of the newfound contact, and once again a little
is sprinkled on the skull. Thus the skull is named, and
gradually the contact is established.

THE SKULL WITHIN THE RITES

The main function of 'the skull within the rites' is that it
serves as a key to sought-after inspirational workings.
Through the skull and from the other side of the grave,

very often there comes that flash of inspiration and knowledge that in one instant lifts the whole of the gathering many steps further along the path. Very often the working aims and ambitions of the group or coven are confirmed as being right. On top of this, new thoughts and ideas seem to be implanted within the collective minds of the group, which not only extend the path being worked but open up other paths as well. In this sense, the spiritual contact becomes or takes on the attributes of the priest-king guide and leader who dwelt within the royal cairn.

In another way, the skull becomes the skull of prophecy. In the past, when the skull was more often used in this way, it would be held in the hands, and questions would be asked of it. If the skull felt lighter, the answer would be 'Yes.' If the skull felt heavier, the answer would be 'No.' Today, instead of its being held in the hands, the skull is placed in the centre of a circle in a darkened room, and questions are put to its spirit contact. Everyone present lets their mind go into a sort of free flow, until the answers start coming through.

To be quite truthful about this, I am not too sure that all these answers are spirit-sent. Just the sheer fact that enough minds are searching for an answer through an external contact may very often enable the answer to be found within themselves. But whatever their origin, the answers come through every time and prove with hindsight to be the correct ones.

There is one other form of skull tradition within the craft, which has been handed on to us from our remote ancestors, though today it is rarely if ever used. This is the totem skull, the animistic symbol of the clan, which gradually evolved into another form of ritual. As such, and as a matter of pure historical interest, I feel that there is a place within these pages for it.

From prehistory onwards, there has been a recognized magical link between the hunter and his prey. Many examples of this link are to be found, ranging from the famous cave painting of the stag-masked, hide-clad god or magician in the Caverne des Trois Frères, Ariège, through to the ritually piled animal bones hidden at the back of caves. Growing from the concept of a sympathetic magical rapport between the hunter and the hunted, through working certain magical rites, the next step would be a gradual recognition of the clan or tribe of the bear, bison, deer or whatever animal was involved. Mixed with the concept of the rites to bring good hunting came the recognition that the fertility of the species being hunted was of prime importance too. Failure of the herds to reproduce meant starvation for the tribe.

With time came change. No longer were the rites performed deep within caves but out in the open and within the circle. As part of the rituals, the now familiar witches' stang would be mounted at the gateway to the circle. But instead of the horned staff as we know it now, it would be a straight pole with the skull of the totem animal mounted on it. Even though life had changed from a hunting one to that of an agricultural and pastoral life, within the cycle of nature and in the fertility of the fields the cult of the Horned God and the Pregnant Goddess still had its place.

Also within this faith was the concept of the sacrificial animal as a thanksgiving to the guardian gods of the herds and flocks, and above all to the Mother Goddess of the earth. Indeed, part of the sacrificial animal was sacred to the gods and burned on the sacred fire. The rest of the sacrifice would be cooked and eaten by the gathering afterwards. It was a sacred feast shared by gods and people. What had been practised deep in the cave was now practised in the open, with a greater involvement by the group or clan in the rites. Even though circumstances and life-style had changed, the concept of fertility had not, except in externals. Instead of good hunting, a good harvest was prayed for.

As the concept of the Goddess and the Old Gods took on a more human-like guise, so the nature of the sacrifice changed. Thus, as life grew more complex and organized, so did the now expanded vision of the gods. Instead of an animal sacrifice, the concept of the human messenger to the gods arose. The gods and the Goddess, having been given a more human character, could be approached only by another human, the departing soul taking the prayers and pleadings of the tribe. As a development parallel with that of the messenger to the gods, but still having the same objects, the strength and well-being of the tribe, arose the sacrifice of the Divine King, whereby the strength of the tribe was vested in one person, not by right of birth or inheritance but by selection. As long as the king was strong and vigorous, so was the tribe. Sacrificed in his prime, the king became the divine companion to the gods, for the good of the tribe.

Later, as time modified this concept, the sacrifice became once again animal, and from this return to the animal sacrifice came the rather interesting concept of the sacrificial scapegoat. The unfortunate animal, having all the sins and evils of the community visited on its head, had to take them before the gods along with its life, as a token of expiation and payment for the lifting of them – a life substituted for that of the king.

Bearing in mind the concept of being able to transfer ills and evil to the sacrificial animal, and at the same time remembering the sacrifice of the Divine King, the idea of the Magister of a coven, as a divinely inspired leader, having to make a blood sacrifice every seventh year becomes clear. As in the case of the sacrifice of the Divine King, the Magister takes the powers of the leader, and for taking these powers a price has to be paid.

For seven years, through the grace of the Lady, the Magister leads the coven. At the end of the seventh year, the price of his rule would be transferred to 'King Ram'. The ram's life would then be offered up to the Goddess, as a substitute for the Magister's own. The sacred portions would be given over to the sacred fire, and the remaining portions would become the sacred feast. The head of the sacrificed ram would then be buried at the site of 'the Bridge between the Two Worlds'. Hence the apron sometimes worn by the Magister as part of his regalia, as in the case of that worn by the other members, symbolizes nothing more than a butcher's apron.

Today, this sacrifice is no longer demanded, and rightly so. Instead, it has been replaced by the oath of office taken and retaken by the Lady and the four officers every seven years. However, one can occasionally find a group that has marked the gateway to the circle with a buried sheep's head as a reminder of the animistic totem spirit of the clan. In the same way, the forked stang or staff is the symbol of the young Horned King of the greenwood and the hunt, the one that stands between the coven and the Mother, the Goddess.

IV The Rituals

1   Beginning the Rituals

These rituals are not an attempt to resurrect the old ways, but a creation based on the old ways. The names, the tools and the symbols are all of the old tradition; but the words and thoughts are tuned to the modern age. Some people will no doubt dismiss them out of hand, while others will scathingly point out that, 'Things aren't done this way. It's not the old tradition.' My answer to these charges is that the working of these rites gives satisfaction. It does create a harmony between the group members, as well as opening up an awareness of both the past and the present. Those of us who have worked them find that they are fulfilling and give an answer to some of our needs and feelings. 'The pearl that is the Lady is the fountainhead of all wisdom.' Who am I to reject what I feel she has sent me?

Before going on, there is one thing that should be made clear. As they are set down at present, all the rituals have been written with a full coven of thirteen in mind. However, anyone desiring to work these rites can adapt them to the number of people taking part.

The other thing that should be borne in mind is that, according to ancient Celtic tradition, it is the site, the place of working, which holds the power, rather than the congregation of people who foregather there. So the solitary person holding up a cup of wine in honour of the Lady and the Old Gods at such a site can gain as much meaning from that simple ritual as a coven of thirteen working the full rites.

One of the reasons for my re-examination of what I had been taught, which led to my writing this book, was the way in which our group split up after Robert Cochrane's death. I felt at the time and I still feel that the Old Mysteries deserve better than the treatment they get even now. The fundamental weakness then, and to a certain degree today, is the importance of the Magister and the Maiden, the male and female leaders respectively, in the group. The trouble is that usually they have been the founding members and leading lights of the coven. The consequence has been that gradually whatever they have said has tended to become coven law, so that when one or the other of them has either left or died, the coven has tended to split up. Basically, the trouble is that the Craft as a faith is so fragmented that total recovery is out of the question. The mansions are still there, but they stand in need of refurbishment.

This does not mean that the past should be rejected out of hand. The Craft is not static but dynamic, yet at the same time firmly rooted in history. For the act of worship is not in the congregation; the sacred place is an end unto itself. By re-invoking the Old Gods, and above all the Goddess, the act of worship can and should relate to the present time, rather than trying to re-create the long lost Golden Age – if in fact there ever was one. Times change, needs change; but the basic truths are still as valid today as they ever were. Unheard for centuries except by a select few, the message still rings down through the corridors of time to be heard by those who have ears and are willing to listen.

Casting the Circle

The history of the magical circle is old, very old. Not only is it a working area but the symbol of eternity, in so far as it has no beginning and no end. By casting the circle, that area becomes *de facto* sacred ground, a defence against hostile forces and containing the energy that forms the cone of power.

Traditionally, the witches' circle is nine feet in diameter; but in the case of a full thirteen or more working the rite, a larger circle is desirable. If the size has to be increased, this is done in multiples of three feet. The one thing that has to be remembered is that no matter how elaborate or simple the circle is, it should be cast and treated with reverence and respect, for it will indeed be sacred ground. Outdoor working is the ideal; but in these present days, unfortunately, it is not always possible.

The actual circle is cast by the officer of the East, even though the invocation is performed by the Lady. To carry out this task East will need certain tools, as well as the means for kindling the sacred fire. He will need the besom, two knives, two short staves or markers for the Gate of the North, and a length of cord half the diameter of the circle being cast.

The first task is to drive one of the knives firmly into the ground where the sacred fire or flame will be. He then ties one end of the cord to it, and the other end is tied to the second knife. Establishing the north by using a compass, and keeping the cord taut, he scribes out the circle, ending up back at north again, where the knife is left stuck in the ground.

The next task is to set up the two markers for the gateway of the north, by sticking them in the earth on the circle's edge and about two feet six inches to three feet apart. He then returns to the centre of the circle and, taking out the knife, builds up the fire ready for lighting. The next job is to coil up the cord and remove the other knife from the circle's edge.

The next step is for East to light the fire. How this is done is up to personal choice. For myself, I use a firelighter and matches; but before lighting, I strike a few symbolic sparks with flint and steel, as a matter of personal feeling.

With the fire burning well, East is then ready to leave the circle. To do this he uses the last of his tools, the besom. This is the bridge between the two worlds, and East takes it to the north with him. He places it across the edge of the circle and between the two markers, with the brush end on the inside. Leaping over it from right to left, he leaves the circle and goes to the Lady. She is waiting outside the circle with the horned stang. East approaches her and bows low.

East: 'The circle is cast according to our way. The fire is lit. All that is needed is for you to enter and call upon Our

Lady and the Guardians to make this ground sacred by
their presence.'

Lady: 'Before you return to the others of our gathering, I
call on you to perform one more task. Take this our altar
and plant it firmly in its accustomed place of usage.'

East, with a bow, takes the stang and plants it about
three feet back from the edge of the circle, so that it is
framed between the two markers when seen from the
inside of the circle. He then returns to the rest of the
gathering, who are some distance away.

The Lady enters the circle by crossing the besom from
left to right, and draws it in after her. She then goes to
each quarter in turn, starting with the east. She crosses her
arms on her breast, bows low and calls on the spirit of that
quarter: 'Be with us and bear witness to our act of
worship.' When she has done this and finished up at the
north, she goes to the fire and for a few moments gives
thought to what she is about to do, before starting the
Invocation of the Circle:

> By stang and cauldron, cup and knife,
> By right of office that I hold,
> Ye ancient powers of death and life,
> Forgather to the circle's fold.
>
> Kinship to kinship, blood to blood,
> By wild night wind and starry sky,
> By heathland brown and darkling wood,
> To this our circle now draw nigh.
>
> In likeness of a henge of stone,
> Stand guard around the circle's rim,
> While looming through the dark alone,
> Stands in the east the Hele-stone dim.
>
> I summon forth the faery hounds,
> Sharp-fanged, white-coated, red of ear,
> To prowl beyond the circle's bounds,
> And put intruders' hearts in fear.
>
> Ancestral powers of this our blood,
> We are your people, guard us well,

By earth and air, by fire and flood,
By magic mime and spoken spell.

Our craft's own Goddess I invoke,
And Ancient Ones of hill and mound.
With fire aflame and drifting smoke,
I dedicate this circle's bound.

By three times three,
Thus shall it be!

The circle dedication rite is one that is rich in
symbology. Looked at closely, it falls into three distinct
parts. In the first section, the Lady invokes by right of
office. After all, she has pledged herself to lead the coven
or group in the service of Our Lady of the Night. The
calling by the stang, cauldron, cup and knife is a reference
to the Horned God and to the Cauldron of Inspiration and
all that it stands for. The cup and knife are of course
symbolic of the male and female aspects of the Old Faith
and the union of the two, as presented in the dedication of
the cakes and wine.

'Kinship to kinship, blood to blood' is an appeal to our
ancestral roots, the kinship of race; for those of us who are
of the old blood very often seem to be attuned to the old
ways and have a goodly share of the Celtic other-
worldliness in our thoughts and feelings.

By creating the mental image of a henge monument as a
working circle, with the hele-stone looming dimly outside
at the east (as at Stonehenge), and by calling on the Lady
of the Night and the Old Lords of both hill and mound,
one can gradually get the feeling that one is reaching back
into time, tuning in to the vibrations and atmosphere of
the country and, for a short span of time, becoming as one
with the hidden spirit of the land.

By calling on the faery hounds, one is calling on the
Hounds of Gwyn ap Nudd, the Wild Hunt, the Gabriel
Hounds or Herne's Hounds, led by the Brindle Bitch, as
he rides the Night Mare. Calling on Gwyn to let them
prowl beyond the circle's edge is calling for a protective
element, keeping all that has no right to enter the circle

away from it. The strange thing is that one not only gets the feeling that they are there: sometimes one can actually see the shadowy forms of them around the circle. Another very strange phenomenon is that very often, for no reason at all, dogs in the area will start barking – and many's the time I've heard it.

By creating what is truly a sanctuary for those who are within the ring, one finds not only a certain quality of peace within the soul but also a wisdom gained through involvement.

Here is another poem which could also be used for the dedication of the circle:

> By magic staff and flame of fire-light,
> Eldest of Gods, we call on ye anew!
> Be present here in all your ancient might,
> Our life in primal nature to renew.
>
> Goddess of witchcraft and the wandering moon,
> Lady of midnight and the starry sky,
> We tread thy dance to seek a magic boon.
> Open the vision of the inward eye!
>
> Lord of the wildwood and the wilderness,
> O Hornéd One, come to thy coven's call!
> Bring us to freedom from the world's duress,
> When night's black cloak is gathered over all.
>
> Now is the circle cast by witch's blade.
> Enter no seen nor unseen enemy!
> Its round is drawn – now be true magic made!
> Our wills are joined – and thus so mote it be!

Dedication of the Cakes and Wine

The dedication of the cakes (or bread) and wine should be treated as the centre point of the main ritual. In its most primitive form, it was the physical partaking of the body of the sacrificed Divine King. In short, it was ritual cannibalism. In the Christianized version, the communion is symbolic of the partaking of the body and blood of the sacrificed Christ and is taken in memory of the Last Supper.

In early Christian theology, the elements of the Eucharist were converted into the body and blood of Christ through the magical act of transubstantiation. Once again, it was the joining-together of the congregation in the partaking of a sacrificial feast. Looking at the taking of the bread and wine in this light, the idea that both elements are charged and magically changed during the actual ritual of blessing is easily understood and recognized for what it is, a partaking of the power of the Goddess. Remember, the cup is the equivalent of the cauldron from which the wisdom and inspiration of the Goddess flow.

There are two ways of dealing with the cup, the bread and the wine. These things can be brought into the circle with the Lady and left at the edge and to the north. The other way is for them to be placed at the foot of the staff and collected by the Lady just before she calls on East to come over and help her with the consecration. For myself, I prefer the latter way, as the Lady goes to the symbol of the Horned God to bring forth the feast, and establishes the link between the Mother, the Horned God and the people.

The Lady leaves the circle and approaches the garlanded staff. Before taking the wine and cakes from the foot of the stang, she bows low and contemplates the significance of the ritual for a few moments. She then bows again and backs away into the circle. Then she puts the cakes and wine down and closes the circle again. The Lady calls East over to her, and while she holds the cup, East fills it with wine. He steps back and draws his knife. The Lady then starts the invocation of the Drawing Down of the Power:

Lady: 'I call upon the Goddess to see this our ritual – to lift the veil between us. For by joining cup and knife, we symbolize the joining of the two elements, for the continuation of life. For this the cup shall be the symbol of the Mother, and the knife shall be the symbol of the Horned God, her lover.'

She raises the cup on high with both hands. East steps

forward and, passing his arms round those of the Lady, raises the knife and holds it in both hands point down above the cup.

East: 'By the symbol of the knife, I call upon the Horned God to join with the Mother in the charging of this cup, so that the wisdom of the ages may mingle with the wine for the benefit of us all.'

He lowers the knife into the cup and at the same time kisses the Lady. The cup is then put to one side. (It can be passed to an assistant to hold for the time being.) The Lady takes the cakes, which are wrapped up in a clean cloth, and brings them to East.

East: 'I call upon the Old Gods to look upon this our sacrifice with pleasure and understanding. For we do this in memory of the past. By the eating of this bread, we take within ourselves the ancient wisdom of the high and lonely places. By the call of blood to blood, we claim the rights of this our heritage.'

He then touches each cake or piece of bread with the knife, saying: 'By cup, by knife and by staff, I bless this our sacred bread.' He may add these verses as a blessing and consecration:

By the virtue of this knife,
Be filled with wisdom and with life!
Grain that Mother Earth doth give,
Sown and reaped that we may live.
So we too in time return

To earth that claimeth all in turn,
Yet as the seed lies hid in earth,
In death is promise of rebirth.
By earth and water, wind and flame,
Be blesséd in the Old Ones' name!

The Lady then carries the wine to each one in turn, and East carries the bread or cakes to them.

Lady: 'With this wine and bread, we renew our pledge to each other, in faith, in love, in harmony. Thus in this way of worship the many become as one.'

It will be noted that either bread or cakes may be used for this ritual, as they are both made of grain, the gift of

Mother Earth which sustains life. Equally, the wine may be of the coven or group's own choosing, though red wine is probably most appropriate, considering the ancient meaning and derivation of the rite.

In Charles Godfrey Leland's book, *Aradia: or the Gospel of the Witches*, in which he recorded the surviving traditions of the witches of Italy, we are told that they held a similar ritual meal, using cakes made from flour, wine, salt and honey, and formed into the shape of a crescent moon. Many present-day witches like to bake the ritual cakes specially in this way. However, if the coven prefers something more primitive, perhaps pieces of wholemeal bread or a favourite local recipe of their own (oatcakes, for instance, in Scotland), it is entirely up to them.

A platter or tray to hold the cakes and wine is a pleasing thing to have as a coven possession. This may be decorated with some suitable design: – for instance, a large pentagram (five-pointed star).

2 The Four Great Sabbats

The first of the four Great Sabbats is Candlemas, held on 2 February. This is the time when traditionally the Wild Hunt rides through the sky on the cold winter blast. But at the same time, it is the season of the year when the first signs of spring begin to appear. Hence the earliest spring flowers, the snowdrops, have the old countryside name 'Candlemas bells'. The month of February gets its name from the Latin *Februarius mensis*, meaning the time of purification, the ancient ritual origin of spring cleaning. It is the time to drive out the spirit of the old year. This is done within the circle, and after the banishing ritual has been performed the site is cleansed with salt.

This is also the time for the ritual planting of one grain of wheat or barley in a large flower-pot, which is then kept by one of the coven appointed to the task. Then, in commemoration of the Wild Hunt, the site is left by running away to the sound of the horn and lots of noise, the wilder the better.

The next Great Sabbat is May Eve, also called Beltane or Walpurgis Night. It takes place on 30 April. It is the time of welcome to the coming summer and the birth of the young Horned King. In olden days, it was celebrated with bonfires, hence its Celtic name of Beltane, meaning 'bright fire'. Walpurgis Night takes its name from an obscure saint called Walburga, who was probably an old nature goddess in Christian guise.

It is the time of planning and starting new things. By now the seed that was ritually planted at Candlemas should be showing signs of sprouting.

The first day of August brings the Sabbat of Lammas. This is the time of thanksgiving for all that the year has brought to the coven. Part of it can be a harvest home ritual as well as a time of contemplation. In some ways, it is a time of sadness for the things that have passed, never to be relived. By now the seed planted in the pot should be ripe and ready for cutting, even as the harvest in the fields. However, it is also the season of 'the Lammas growth', when the old sacred oak trees of Britain put forth a new young growth of leaves. It was among such oak trees in the New Forest 'on the morrow of Lammas' that the Red King, William Rufus, met a mysterious and perhaps sacrificial death.

When the coven's ritual ear of wheat or barley is cut, if any member so chooses, they can take one of the seeds from the ear and grow it at home as a private symbol of worship, using it as a key for the focus of the mind.

Hallowe'en on 31 October is the Sabbat that everyone has heard about. It is the old Samhain Eve, the Celtic festival of the beginning of winter. The bright orange-coloured pumpkins are ripe and ready for making into traditional Hallowe'en lanterns by hollowing them out, roughly cutting a goblin face on them and putting a lighted candle inside. On Samhain Eve all sorts of uncanny creatures were supposed to walk abroad, and like Beltane six months earlier it was an occasion for bonfires and merrymaking.

It is actually the ancient pagan festival of remembering and communicating with the dead. On this occasion only are the twin circles laid out, one for the living and one for the dead. The ritual crosses from one circle to the other, and as part of the ritual the members of the coven can light a candle for anyone they would like to remember. These candles are used instead of a sacred fire in the centre of the circle for the dead.

It will be seen that these four Great Sabbats occur at regular intervals of roughly three months. Between them occur the Lesser Sabbats of the spring and autumn equinoxes and the summer and winter solstices. Of these, Midsummer in particular was an ancient time of festival, and the solstice of Midwinter was better known as Yule, which people today celebrate as Christmas. The date of Easter depends upon the first full moon after the spring equinox, which shows it to have been originally a pagan festival of spring.

The four Great Sabbats should be kept by the whole coven. However, the equinoxes (about 21 March and 21 September) and the solstices (about 21 June and 21 December) may be celebrated as a coven gathering or by working at home with your partner. If a person has no working partner, he or she can work on their own indoors or out. The actual date of the equinoxes and solstices may vary a little each year, for astronomical reasons. This can be checked in most popular astrological magazines.

Fasting and Purification

By tradition, before any of the four major rituals of Candlemas, May Eve, Lammas and Hallowe'en, there should be a period of fasting for the twenty-four hours preceding the rite. In the case of any serious magical working the same rule should be observed. How strictly this is observed by any group or coven is a matter for the membership to decide.

In the case of my old group, it depended on the physical efforts entailed at work by the individual member. In the case of an office worker, no harm should come from a total abstinence, but a blacksmith or foundry worker who missed out on salt intake would soon find themselves feeling very ill. In the rite of fasting, common sense should dictate the severity of the regime.

So what should be given up for the rite? Theoretically, everything except water; but in most cases it now involves the giving-up of meat, fish, vegetables, alcohol and salt. Toast with a boiled egg is acceptable for those who feel the need to eat. Tea and coffee are acceptable too, providing of course that moderation is observed. In my case, as a heavy tea-drinker, just cutting down on tea takes a strong act of will. To give it up all together, I'd need an anaesthetic!

Behind the concept of the ritual fast is a twofold aim. Firstly, the act of fasting takes an effort of strong will-power. That same will-power also has its purpose within the circle. Secondly, it develops the power to overlook the pangs of hunger and the things of the outer world, while at the same time bringing the total mental energy of the individual to bear on the magical working being done.

To develop the will whereby bodily discomfort can be and is ignored, and eventually left behind, means that the spirit or soul is free from this earthly existence and able to respond to the flow of the force or power raised within the circle during the rite. Also, part of the aim of the fast is to create a certain amount of disorientation within the body. Once, the fast, coupled with certain drugs, was used to obtain this end. Today we know better. Drugs within the magical circle belong more to the age of the shaman-priest than to the modern witch.

Today the trance-like, out-of-this-body experience is brought about by an act of will. Thus, by the powers of the will and the divorcing of the psyche from the body, the initiate gains the state of 'spinning without motion between two worlds'. For that period of time, the circle becomes the centre of the universe, with the firmament seemingly revolving round it. It is the world that is part of neither the heavens nor the earth. It is the world of dreams, illusions – and finally, when illusion becomes reality, truth.

Coupled with this disorienting of the body, and as part of the process, is the circle chant. Just as a piece of music can express emotions [as for instance the music of 'Mars, the Bringer of War', from Holst's suite called *The Planets* – listening to it, there can be no mistaking its meaning], so it is with the circle chant. The tempo of the chant, along with the breathing-control brought about by it, creates changes within the body. Coupled with the fast and the altered oxygen levels in the bloodstream, all these things combine to bring about the mental state of other-worldliness that should be the first stage in a successful magical working. Whereas the shaman-priest of old used drugs and the sacred dance to reach a state of heightened ecstasy and communion with the gods, the modern witch does it by an act of will and through knowledge, in order to seek some small measure of understanding of life, the gods, and the spiritual relationship between the self and the Goddess.

In some ways, this disorientation of the physical self in

the same controlled manner is the key to the projected magical spell. In this case, though, the coven chant and the Treading of the Mill are the same as the opening-up to the Goddess. By the fixing of the aims or ends that are being worked for within the collective minds of the gathering, the forces or powers raised within the circle are willed or directed at the required target, be it for good or evil, healing or harm.

Once again, it should be stressed that the ritual fast is part of the working rite. As such, it should be used as only part of the working rite or magical spell-making. In the case of most of the full moon Esbats that fall within the ritual year cycle, these are nothing more than acts of worship. In these instances, there is no need for the ritual fast, as the aims of the rites are different. Instead, they are a joining-together of kindred souls in a communion with the Goddess and the Old Gods, as in the sixteenth-century verse quoted by T.C. Lethbridge in his book *Witches: Investigating an Ancient Religion*:

> Diana and her darling crew shall pluck your fingers fine,
> And lead you forth right pleasantly to sup the honey wine.
> To sup the honey wine, my loves, and breathe the heavenly air,
> And dance, as the young angels dance. Ah, god, that I were there!

In the words of the old, old greeting, 'Merry meet and merry part, and merry meet again!' To have done this, and then to lose it in later years, means that forever in your heart there is that longing to recapture the past moments spent within the witches' circle, under a clear, star-spangled, moon-lit sky. This is the time when the Goddess takes part of your soul and makes it forever hers.

Because of the nature of things, and a magical working being what it is, there is always a need to earth a ritual. In this sense, just as you try to leave behind the things of this world when entering the circle, so the reverse has to be done when leaving the circle; in short, some sort of ritual purification and earthing, or literally bringing the senses back to earth. In most cases, this means just doing something mundane, such as having a few beers to release post-working tension. Or should you have a working partner who is willing and feels the same as you do, sex is very often used as the stabilizing influence. Though this may sound a cold-blooded way of putting it, the emotions involved between a working couple are most certainly not cold-blooded. Because of the intimate and trusting relationship that builds up between them, the joining-together in the act of sex is really a joining-together in an act of love, and perhaps a more fitting climax to any meeting.

This is not or ever has been an excuse for an orgy. If people wish to indulge in this sort of thing, by all means do so; but don't dress it up as an act of worship to the Goddess. To join together in love and respect is a private matter, done in private, and no concern of anyone else. To join together in lust in an orgiastic way is not part of the faith.

In the same light, very often working a heavy ritual or perhaps by not earthing a rite properly, there is a feeling that an individual or a group is being bogged down in a sea of black depression – or, to put it in another way, suffering from 'bad vibes'. Also, and far too often, you have the individual who pushes himself or herself too far and in the end becomes damaged and disillusioned. Very often in cases of this sort, a cold shower in the form of a purification or the leaving-behind of past events is called for.

If a group or coven is ever called on to work the rite of a formal cursing or banishment, this can often leave the group feeling drained, unsettled and in a state of disharmony. This is where the rite of purification is at its most useful, because in effect it is the means of turning a personal or collectively felt guilt into a rite and act of expiation. Should the group as a whole feel the need for this, as part of the rite the fast ought to be observed.

How simple or complicated this rite is to be, once again it is a matter for the group or coven to decide upon. The rite itself can range from simple sprinkling with consecrated water, to the exceedingly formal and complicated Great Rite of Purification.

With the most simple form of purification, once again this is done in a fully charged and consecrated circle. It needs a bowl of water and a small bundle of twigs, bound at one end to form a handle. As water is to be sprinkled around, this rite is usually held out of doors; but if it can be held inside, and if people feel that they would like it to be held inside, by all means do so. The thing that has to be remembered is that this is a ritual working and not a ceremonial working. So the circle is a fully charged and consecrated circle and accordingly laid out with the full circle rites. No matter if it is only one person or the whole group undergoing purification, the rite is the same in all cases.

The Officer of the East, or whoever is laying out the circle, brings the bowl into the ring, leaving it by the fire after the latter has been lit. The actual water is in the care of West, and he is the one who brings this into the circle.

With everyone gathered inside and the circle closed, the Lady, in the aspect or guise of a priestess of the Goddess, instead of taking her usual position in the north, stands by the fire, with everyone gathered round her in a circle. On this occasion she does not open with the Sangreal Prayer. Instead she uses something more suitable for the occasion, because the group is asking not for knowledge or inspiration but rather for something to be lifted and taken from them. So she speaks thus:

Lady: 'I call upon the Old Gods and guardians of this our gathering ... to see and understand the burden that is upon us ... And in the realizing ... take from us the cause of our disharmony ... Where once a blood price would be paid for this absolving ... Water, without which none can live, is offered in its place ... The symbol of the forgetfulness and oblivion of the timeless river ... to wash away the discord from our souls and bring harmony in its place.'

After a few moments' silence, the Lady calls West to join her in the centre of the circle. West, handing the bottle or flask of water to her, picks up the bowl for the Lady to pour it into.

Lady: 'By the powers granted to me as a priestess of the

Goddess ... I charge this water with the sacred powers invoked for the washing clean of the soul.'

She puts the bottle or flask down and, taking the bowl from West, raises it on high as she would the cup during the charging of the wine. West then draws his knife, raises it and lowers the point into the water, at the same time saying:

West: 'Thus with the act of joining knife to water, symbolizing the joining of the Goddess as the Young Maid with the Young Horned King ... So the water in this vessel shall be charged with the powers of the sacred blood of sacrifice ... to pay the price for the removal of the burdens that are upon us.'

He kisses the Lady. Sheathing his knife, he takes the bowl from her. The Lady takes the twig brush and dips it into the water. Flicking a few drops first upon herself and then on West, she proceeds to do the same to the rest of the gathering, using the words:

Lady: 'Thus with this lustration, given in the knowledge of the rightness of our act ... I wash away from us that which has brought disharmony ... In this token rite of washing, shall be the knowledge that all that has gone before is now taken from us ... leaving us as the newly washed babe ... cleansed in both body and soul ... and once again ready to work the mysteries of our faith.'

There is a short pause, and then the Lady goes on to say:

Lady: 'As for the charged water that is left ... From the earth it came ... To the earth I return it ... In the name of the Goddess ... So be it done.'

Effectively the rite is now over; but should the group feel that they would like to perform a token ring dance, dancing deosil as a way of winding things down, by all means do so. Remember, however, that because of the nature of the rite there is no feast afterwards. The leaving of the circle marks the closing of the rite.

The Royal Cairn

The royal cairn is nothing more than a piece of symbolism. In some ways, it is an empty expression of tenets of faith and belief. Yet in the simple act of creating the cairn, it becomes a physical expression of a complex theology.

So what is the royal cairn? In short, nothing more than a pile of stones carried to the working site by the members. Behind the act of carrying a stone to the site and leaving it there is the concept that every member attending the meeting carries with them burdens from this world. By their leaving the stones in a pile, it symbolizes the leaving-behind of the cares of this world before entering the sacred circle of the Goddess. By leaving the stone behind, you are saying in effect, 'I leave my cares in the lap of the Goddess.'

On another level, by bringing the stones and creating, over a period of time, a mound, the group or coven is creating the equivalent of the royal grave. In a mystical sense, the king never dies. Though the body dies, the bloodline still continues through the child, who in turn becomes the father of the next heir. The king in effect was the servant of the gods, as well as being a physical symbol or expression of the strength and well-being of the group, clan or tribe. In terms of sympathetic magic, if the king was allowed to weaken through age or infirmity, so would the strength of his clan or tribe weaken.

In fact, most early civilizations used to take this so seriously that the king had to go through a sort of royal stamina test. In ancient Egypt, it was the Heb-Sed ceremony, where the Pharaoh would have to run a fixed distance. In earlier times, the king would be the Divine Sacrifice, killed in his prime for the good of the tribe. From this sacrifice came the tradition of the seven-year reign. At the end of seven years, the king either died or sacrificed a substitute. Today, besides being illegal, the blood sacrifice is totally unnecessary and recognized as such. In its place, the seven-year oath of office has been substituted.

When the Divine King died on May Eve and his successor donned his mantle, the blood from the sacrifice would be collected in a bowl. A few drops of the blood would be mixed with ale, mead or, later in time, wine. A libation of this draught would be poured to the Great Earth Mother, and the rest would be drunk by the priesthood. In this way, part of the royal divinity would be absorbed by the priesthood. In a sense, this acted as the token cannibalistic feast.

The rest of the blood royal would be mixed with water and sprinkled over the gathering of the people, using small bunches of birch twigs. Birch, being the symbol of birth and rebirth, symbolized the death and resurrection cycle, while the drops of blood and water represented the last blessing of the now dead king to his people. The man who gave his life for the good of his people would still be with them beyond the grave. Parts of the body would then be buried in the surrounding fields, as the symbol of the son returning to the Mother's womb. They would bring with them the virility of the late king to fertilize the seed within the earth.

The final part of the ceremony, or perhaps better to say the sacred drama, would be when a priest and priestess earthed the ritual by copulating in the field. This was a sympathetic magical act to enhance the fertility of the crops, and one that was carried out each year irrespective of whether or not that year was the one of the sacrifice of the Divine King.

To the priesthood, remembering that the Divine King would for his term of office be a member and leader of that priesthood, the pile of stones which marked the royal grave would become the home on earth of the soul or spirit of the Divine Sacrifice. The grave containing the skull and bones of the king would be a place of reverence to the ordinary people, the hallowed bones making the burial mound a sacred place; so much so that other remains would be buried in the sides of the mound, in the hope that the remains and therefore the shade of that person would in some small way come to share part of the divinity of the dead king. In the meantime, the priesthood would call back the soul of the departed kings by magical means, to the home on earth built by the priesthood. There, through trance mediumship, the collective souls of the priest-kings would be invoked, to help, advise and protect the people they died for, until rebirth brought them back to this world again. Not only was the king a messenger to the gods on behalf of the people, he was also the sympathetic ear beyond the grave.

The actual cairn itself would also act as an identifying point to the reborn soul of the Divine King, much in the same way as the sacred articles that are used to help locate the reborn soul of a Buddhist lama. A small child who seems to recognize and pick out these things is examined and tested to see if he is an old soul in a young body. Thus the pile of stones would be recognizable to the reborn soul, because many of the stones would represent the earthly burdens carried and left at the sacred site by the king in a past life.

Over a period of years, time would modify some of these ideas and meanings, and in some cases change the concept all together. New waves of invaders, bringing their own gods, ideas and forms of worship, would either drive the worship of the native gods underground or bring it in line with that of their own deities. At the same time, there would be this recognition that these places were special and marked out as sacred spots. In time, they would tend to become the places of meeting, mounds of pronouncement and judgment by the priesthood.

Gradually, however, the function of the piles of stones became lost along with their meaning. Instead of the site being known as a sacred area, it became just another place to clear and plant, and the little piles of stones were scattered. As the tribal kingdoms grew bigger, so did the centres of worship. Instead of being simple places of worship, they either died out or evolved into more grandiose and complex centres of religion, as well as becoming physical extensions of tribal pride.

In some ways the decline was similar to that of the Christian Church. The cathedrals and parish churches have survived and are still being used; but how many of the little wayside shrines have survived? If they are marked on the map at all, it is just as 'The site of ...'.

The concept and creation of the royal cairn as marking a meeting-place suffered other blows, with the secrecy of the Old Faith during the times of persecution. The little pile of stones would be a dead give-away as to what was going on there. Another blow was (and still is) the lack of privacy. How many groups actually own their own site? To work in the same place all the time and create the cairn is fine – providing, of course, the group owns the meeting-place or is permitted to use it by a willing owner. For those of us who are able to do so, however, the symbolic royal cairn and the concept behind it are most certainly worth re-creating.

Today the royal cairn should be treated as a purely symbolic creation. No longer are the stones regarded as the resting-place for the shade of the sacrificed Divine King. Instead it becomes a place for the leaving of burdens – the place where all cares and arguments are left behind. From the place of the stones to the place of the circle, the walk should be a silent one, when the individual is preparing the mind for the coming rite.

Each person who will be at the meeting should find themselves a fist-sized stone or pebble to carry to the site. When they reach the meeting-area, all the stones are placed on the pile with a short prayer: 'With this stone, I leave behind all the cares of this world. With the shedding of these cares, may the Goddess find me in a fit and proper state to do Her worship.' When the stone is placed on the pile, the feelings and emotions of this world should be left behind. From this moment on, each individual will be a worshipper of the Goddess, dealing with the things of her world and her circle, rather than the things of their own.

Sometimes, if a member is ill, some other member as a special favour can take a stone to take up to the site for them. In doing this, what in effect is being said is, 'Though I'm not there in person, my problems are being taken to the lap of the Goddess, and left there for her to help me overcome.' In another sense, the mound of stones is a private memorial to all those who have worked with the group over the years. Though they may no longer be there in a physical way, the stones they brought are in a way part of them, the little something of themselves that they have chosen to leave behind.

In this sense, the empty grave can be as empty or as full of meaning as a group or coven wishes to make it. It can be just a meaningless piece of ritual, or it can mean that a person does in fact leave something behind with the stone and then goes forward to the working-place feeling that they have really left behind the cares of this world before entering the sacred circle.

Quite a few people will say that the royal cairn is not really part of the Craft, and in this I must agree with them. Traditionally, it is not part of the Craft, but rather a concept that we rediscovered and decided to make our own. As I have said before, in the creating of the cairn there is a meaning and there is an expression or idea to be found. In some ways, the pile of stones itself, no matter how big or small, is the meeting-place of kindred souls. It is the gateway to the sacred precinct before the actual circle and, as such, the place to leave behind the things of this world.

In another sense, in its creating there is a statement of faith. No longer are you as a group prepared to sneak out hidden by night to work your rites. You have proclaimed your place of worship and marked it with the symbol of the empty grave. Beyond this grave is to be found the rose from the wastelands that have been made to bloom.

Candlemas (2 February)

The Candlemas ritual should be held outdoors. But if the usual working place is indoors, the actual rite of cleansing is held there, while the feast, weather permitting, can be held outside with a brief token ritual and the Wild Hunt re-enacted afterwards. But as the chase across country is not germane to the actual rite, but more of a way of 'letting off steam', it can be omitted all together.

One other thing to note is that when the full coven form up on the outside of the circle, they do so in the order of male–female, omitting the Lady from this pattern. After the coven members are in position, the Lady joins the group, taking her position at the south as shown in the illustration. From there she leads off deosil (clockwise), tapping each person on the shoulder as she passes. They fall in behind her one after the other, until she has paced right round the circle and returned to her position in the south. She then goes on round to the north and enters the circle by crossing the bridge there.

From the illustration it can be seen that by forming up in

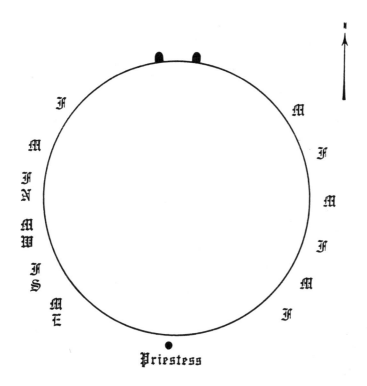

Priestess

this way all the officers of the four quarters will be in their correct order. Directly behind the Lady will be East (male), South (female), West (male) and North (female).

The Lady reaches the twin posts or gateway into the circle and jumps across the besom which forms the 'bridge'. Holding both hands out, she helps each of the officers into the circle. Each in turn makes an obeisance to her by touching their foreheads to her hands, before letting go of them and going to their stations. The rest of the coven do the same, before going on to greet and be greeted by each of the four officers in turn, starting with East and finishing with North. They then move to positions round the central fire, leaving gaps for the four officers to join them and form the male–female circle. The Lady then completes the circle by stationing herself in the north, while the rest join hands.

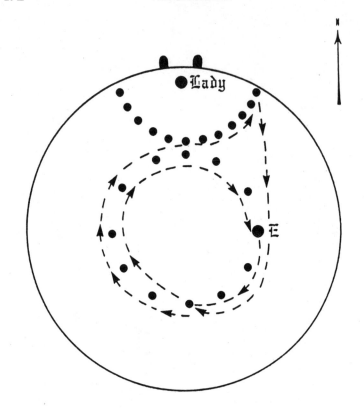

This same method of forming up is to be used for the starting of every ritual.

When everyone is in position, the Lady starts off the ritual with the opening prayer:

Lady: Beloved Bloodmother of my especial breed,
    Welcome me at this moment with your willing womb.
    Let me learn to live in love with all you are,
    So my seeking spirit serves the Sangreal.

The Lady pauses for a few moments to let the thoughts raised by this prayer fix themselves in the people's minds.

Lady: 'As winter precedes summer, so darkness is before light. Before the small young flame can be kindled, the ashes of the old fire must be cleared away. The hopes and fears of the old year grew from a tiny spark, blossomed into fullness and with time died. Only the embers remain in the darkness, waiting to be pushed into the shadows.'

Coven: 'We hear this, we know this, we await this. As the cold wind of the north blows strong, so shall it carry the dust of the past upon its gusts. From the dark north it shall come into the light, and then into the dark it shall go, clearing all before it.'

The Lady, carrying a small bag of salt, goes to each quarter, starting with the east. She scatters a little of the salt around, at the same time saying:

Lady: 'With this salt I banish all that has gone on here before. As in the past our ancestors did sow a site with salt, wherein no man dared dwell, thus we do likewise. With this salt I re-dedicate this area to the Mother our Lady, and in her name do declare anew this area to be sacred.'

She does this at each quarter, and when she has finished she returns to the north, where she faces the circle, saying:

Lady: 'In the name of the Mother, it is thus done.'

Coven: 'In our Lady's name, so be it.'

At this stage, the sacred flame is put out or covered, and a pause of about five minutes is allowed for thought, before the second part of the ceremony is carried out.

By raising her head and crossing her hands over her bosom, the Lady gives the signal to East to rekindle the fire or flame.

East: 'As this flame grows and drives back the dark of night, so may the shadows of unknowing be driven back. May the tiny flicker of hope be fanned into the strong fire of certainty. May the purifying flame burn out the uncertainties of our souls, and replace them with wisdom – and through wisdom, knowledge; the knowledge of what we should be, other than what we are.'

Coven: 'Thus we pray that it shall be. For the pearl that is the Lady is the fountainhead of all wisdom. For it is the words of that wisdom that bring us forward into the light – the light that delivers us from the inner darkness of ourselves, and illuminates the path we tread. Thus as the sun drives back the cold and darkness of winter, so may the light now kindled burn within us, that we may take life as it is and live it in love for what we are.'

The Lady then calls East to her. He approaches her and bows low.

East: 'We are ready and waiting on your command.'

Lady: 'Then bring the others forth to join us in our final act of worship.'

East returns to the rest of the coven and leads them off deosil to where they eventually form a half-circle around the Lady. All but East kneel down. East goes to the side of the circle and collects an earth-filled flower-pot. He brings it back into the half-circle and then kneels in front of the Lady.

Lady: 'Brothers and sisters of the circle, we are gathered here for our final act of worship. What we do now as a physical act is symbolic of what we join together in the circle to do.'

At this point East picks up the flower-pot and holds it out to her. She takes her knife and holds it up. Then she lowers it gently, makes a small hole in the soil of the pot and plants a grain of wheat in it.

Lady: 'As this seed is planted in the soil, may the ideas of our faith be planted in the fertile soil of our minds. There the seed shall germinate and in its time grow towards the light. There, warmed by the light, it shall burst forth in all its splendour.'

West at this point steps forward with a bow and hands the Lady a flask of water. She takes it and holds it on high. West returns to his place.

Lady: 'With the waters of life I bless this seed. For without those waters there can be no life.'

She sprinkles water on the soil, and then blows gently over it three times.

Lady: 'As life is breathed into us, so shall I breathe life into this our symbol, in the name of the Mother.'

She takes the pot from East and places it at her feet.

Lady: 'Within this pot lies the whole cycle of life. From the dark of the Mother's womb we are born into the light. Young life is vigorous, reaching forth like us in our youth, willing to grasp life with both hands. As this seed ripens, so do we in our maturity reach peace and tranquillity. Then in the time of old age, death itself will claim us, and we shall in our own time cross the waters of oblivion and be reborn again.'

At this, all stand up, and once again East leaves the line to get the wine-cup and the cakes and take them to the

Lady. The two of them consecrate the wine with the knife in the usual manner. After this is done, the cakes are blessed in the usual way. With the Lady leading with the cup, and East bearing the cakes, they go round to each member of the group in turn. The Lady gives each one a sip of wine, saying the words:

Lady: 'With this wine we renew our pledge to each other, in faith, in love, in harmony. Thus in this way the many become as one in worship.'

East then gives each member a piece of cake, saying:

East: 'In this symbol we remind ourselves that we eat of the Mother and her offspring, in that the seed must die that we may live, and that in time our mortal shell in turn must become as one with the earth. For in the act of death is the promise of rebirth.'

When all have been served and the Lady and East have finished what is left, a few minutes' silence is observed, to give people time to think a little. East then returns to his position on the right and leads the group back in line to form a circle round the fire once again. Then they all link hands ready to start the next part of the ritual.

The Lady, still standing in the north, folds her hands across her bosom, that being the signal for the people in the circle to start slowly pacing round deosil, using the coven chant. Here is a version of one chant to the Triple Goddess which I have used and found to work very well in the past:

Her three faces we have known,
The Maiden, the Bride and the ancient Crone,
Demanding her due in the ring of stone.
The Hunter, the Stag, the Boar we become,
For Hunter and Hunted are but one.

Three days, three nights, I lay capped with stone,
Till past did present and future join,
Shaping a bridge the worlds to span.
The Hunter, the Stag, the Boar we become,
For Hunter and Hunted are but one.

Three mystic worlds the bridge must span,
From earth to spirit, to the Shining One,

> To return again from whence we came,
> And tread the spiral path again.
> The Hunter, the Stag, the Boar we become,
> For Hunter and Hunted are but one.

With all the coven chanting this and treading out the beat, the Lady decides when it is time to finish. She moves forward and touches East on the shoulder. She then returns to her place in the north. East continues round one more time and then, while still holding on with his right hand to the person behind him, he leads everyone out of the circle, past the Lady and back to the positions they were in before the start of the ritual. The Lady then leaves the circle and returns to her position in the south, with the words:
Lady: 'Brothers and sisters of the circle, the rite is now done, and so to the feast.'

The food and drink are then brought out, and everyone joins in and has a good time.

May Eve (30 April)

This is the time of enjoyment and pleasure. It has a light-hearted approach, as a thanksgiving for what we receive from the circle. Not all circle workings are of a serious nature. Just as life is enjoyable, so the circle workings should reflect this.

The order for starting the May Eve ritual is the same as for all the other rites. For this ritual, the staff or stang is placed just outside the circle and to the north. For this occasion, it should be garlanded with a mixture of birch, hawthorn and willow catkins. If these cannot be obtained, other greenery can be used in their place. At the foot of the staff a small bowl, or better still a cauldron, is placed. In the cauldron is a mixture of milk, honey and vinegar or some other bitter-tasting liquid.

All the members of the group are brought into the circle in the usual manner, and greet each of the four officers by bowing over their hands. They form up in the middle of the circle around the fire and link hands. The Lady completes the circle and turns inwards to face the group. The Lady starts the ritual with the opening Sangreal prayer:

Lady: Beloved Bloodmother of my especial breed,
      Welcome me at this moment with your willing
      womb.
      Let me learn to live in love with all you are,
      So my seeking spirit serves the Sangreal.

The Lady pauses for a few moments to let the thoughts raised by this prayer fix themselves in the people's minds. She then continues:

Lady: 'Brothers and sisters of the circle, once again we are gathered here in our sacred place, to do worship to Our Lady and the Old Gods of both hill and mound. Hidden from the world are they, and hidden shall be our worship.'

Coven: 'Thus away from the sight of others shall we work the mysteries of our chosen path.'

Lady: 'Tonight is a night of joy, for we welcome the returning summer. The young King of the Greenwood is reborn, with the promise of strength and fertility. The seed planted in the dark of the winter is now strong with young life. The Lady is no longer the Mother, but the Young Maid awaiting her chosen one. For by their joining the age-old cycle of life, with its promise of birth and rebirth, shall be fulfilled. Let the greenwoods sing their song of life, for that very spirit of life is strong within us.'

Coven: 'I'O Robin! I'O Marian! Join us, inspire us and help us to cast off that to which we were born and then moulded to. Help us to be as nature meant us, and not as we are now!'

Lady: 'Let the dance begin!'

At these words, everyone begins dancing round the circle deosil. Instead of the usual steady pace of the Mill, a more lively form of dance is used. One of the best beats for this dance is the old folk-tune 'The Lincolnshire Poacher'. It can be whistled, hummed or played on a recorder by a musically minded member of the group. The dance is kept up until the members of the coven are out of breath and in a state of mild euphoria. The Lady then stops the dance and gives everyone a breather, before calling East over to her to dedicate the cakes and wine. This is done in the usual manner, with the wine being consecrated first and the cakes blessed after. The rest of the coven form up in a half-circle around the two of them, and the Lady goes with the cup to each member in turn and offers them a sip of the wine, with the words:

Lady: 'With this wine we renew our pledge to each other, in faith, in love, in harmony. Thus in this way do the many become as one in worship.'

East gives each member a piece of cake, saying:

East: 'With this symbol we remind ourselves that we eat of the Mother and her offspring, in that the seed must die that we may live, and that in time our mortal shell in turn must become as one with the earth. For in the act of death is the promise of rebirth.'

When all have been served, and the Lady and East have finished what is left, there will be a few minutes' silence to give everyone a chance to think a little. Then East leads everyone back to their positions round the fire. The Lady speaks:

Lady: 'Together we have danced the joyous dance. Together we have broken bread and drunk the wine in comradeship. For in this ritual we ask for nothing. We only come to give – to give of our hearts and of ourselves. Our reward is the pleasure of the giving of ourselves to this our circle, and those who join us to work within it.'

Coven: 'We do this freely, for the price of belonging is to give of oneself.'

East: 'What of the potion that lies before the altar, Lady?'

Lady: 'A reminder to us all that within the milk of the Mother is the sweetness of life mingled with the bitterness of disappointment. Thus a balance is struck. For the good on one hand is countered by the sorrows on the other. For by placing them at the foot of the altar, within the cauldron, we accept this of the gods and draw a measure of wisdom from it.'

Coven: 'So be it, and we accept it.'

The Lady then gives the signal to East, who leads the coven around the circle deosil and then out of the ring. Instead of forming up as usual, they all wait in a half-circle outside for the Lady to leave. She does this and then, picking up the cauldron from the foot of the staff, she moves forward a few paces, holding it waist high. She empties the cauldron on the ground, and before putting it back she shows that it is empty.

Lady: 'Thus the cauldron is empty, a symbol of the year to come. For we shall fill it with shared experience, and from its filling draw knowledge and wisdom. But enough of serious thought! Let joy reign, and our watchword be "Do as thou wilt, but harm none." Come, who will play Robin and Marian, and preside over our feast?'

The couple who are willing to do this should volunteer beforehand. When asked, they should step forward, to be crowned with garlands as the king and queen of the woodland glade. In that guise toasts are drunk to them and they are pledged as presiding over the feast.

Lammas (1 August)

This is the time of thanksgiving, the time of mature contemplation for the past year's work. The seeds of that working should be looked at, and thanks given for whatever has been achieved. It is also the time of sorrow, for the season of growth is over and the year must surely die.

The ritual is started by all the members being brought into the circle in the usual manner, and the Lady taking up her position in the north and standing apart from the others.

Instead of East being the main mover of the ritual, this is done by the Lady of the South.

South: 'Brothers and sisters of the circle, before beginning our ritual let us give pause for thought. Think back and remember the dark of the year, the time when we cleansed our circle and planted the seed within the pot. This seed has now grown and flourished. Now is the time to cut and harvest it.'

Coven: 'We know this, and fully understand the meaning behind the symbol.'

South: 'Remember those words and actions of the Lady, who, with the aid of the Lord of the East, planted the seed within the pot. As this symbol was so planted, may the ideals of our faith be planted in the fertile soil of our minds.'

Coven: 'We remember well the spoken prayer.'

South: 'Remember too that the Lord of the West did bring water, and that the Lady did sprinkle the soil with that water, saying, "With the waters of life I bless this seed, for without these waters there can be no life." '

Coven: 'We remember well both word and deed.'

South: 'Remember well when the Lady breathed life into the seed with the words, "As life is breathed into us, so shall I breathe life into this our symbol." '

Coven: 'We recall all that was done in the Mother's name, and the thoughts beyond the actions.'

South: 'I now call upon the Lady to enter the circle, to do that which has to be done.'

At this call the circle is broken for the Lady to enter. She picks up the pot with the stalk of wheat or barley in it and enters the circle. Everyone then joins hands behind her. She places the pot on the ground by the sacred fire and takes one pace backwards. Then, drawing her knife, she holds it point up with both hands, saying:

Lady: 'Thus the Mother in all her guises we have seen. The Maid receiving the seed of the Old King within her. The Mother nurturing that seed within herself. The Aged One as the seed grew to its fullness.'

She then kneels, takes the stalk of grain in her left hand and, with the knife in her right, cuts the stalk through with one sweep of the knife, saying:

Lady: 'Thus the rite is done, the price paid, the sacrifice taken. But from this now dead ear shall spring new life, and each of you will in time take one seed from it. Plant it in your own homes, watch it grow, and then bring back to this our circle the seed from its growing.'

Coven: 'As with the symbol of the seed, so may we take away with us some small part of the wisdom of the Mother. Let it grow within us, so that in time we may return it from whence it came, to share with the others of our circle.'

Lady: 'Now that all is done, I return to the place that is my station.'

The circle around her then breaks open to let her pass through, and everyone rejoins hands. The Lady returns to the north and faces inwards. Just before signalling to the Lady of the South to carry on with the rite, she says the Sangreal Prayer, as this is special to her only:

Beloved Bloodmother of my especial breed,
Welcome me at this moment with your willing womb.
Let me learn to live in love with all you are,
So my seeking spirit serves the Sangreal.

After a pause for a few moments for thought, she gives South the signal to continue by crossing her hands on her breast.

South: 'For a few moments let us tread the measured tread of the Mill. Let us open ourselves to the Mother. For only by the opening of ourselves can we receive that which is ours by right of worship.'

The coven unlink hands and start pacing the Mill, either using the circle chant (as given in the Candlemas ritual on p. 175) or fixing the pace of the movement with the chant of: 'EEE ... YAY ... YOO ... AHH.' This is kept up until the Lady of the South feels that it is time to stop.

When the Mill is done and everyone has got their breath back, the Lady calls on East to come to her and help her to consecrate the cakes and wine in the usual manner. The rest of the coven are formed up in the usual half-circle around them both. The Lady goes to each in turn, giving them a sip of the wine with the words:

Lady: 'With this wine we renew our pledge to each other, in faith, in love, in harmony. Thus in this way do the many become as one in worship.'

East gives each member a piece of cake, saying:

East: 'With this symbol we remind ourselves that we eat of the Mother and her offspring, in that the seed must die that we may live, and that in time our mortal shell must become as one with the earth; for in the act of death is the promise of rebirth.'

When all have been served, and the Lady and East have finished what is left, there is a pause for a few moments, giving everyone a chance to think a little. Then South leads everyone back to their positions around the circle. All stand still for a few moments in silence before the Lady speaks:

Lady: 'Once more, brothers and sisters of the circle, let us tread the dance. Only this time let it be one of joy and understanding. Let us leave this place of our thanksgiving with a feeling of happiness in our hearts, a feeling of well-being for the work that we have done together. My Lady of the South, let the dance begin!'

The dance is led off deosil, and at a pace faster than the one used for the Mill. Should the coven wish, a chant can be used to get the timing. Once again, a good tune to use is the old folk-tune 'The Lincolnshire Poacher'.

Doreen Valiente wrote some words to this tune, which were first published in her book *Witchcraft for Tomorrow*. They are reproduced here:

Come join the dance, that doth entrance,
And tread the circle's round.
Be of good cheer, that gather here,
Upon this merry ground.
Good luck to we that faithful be,
And hold our craft so dear,
For 'tis our delight of a shiny night,
In the season of the year.
Oh, 'tis our delight of a shiny night,
In the season of the year.

While stars do shine, we pledge the wine
Unto the gods of old.
Nor shall there fail the witch wassail,
Nor shall their fire grow cold.
Good luck to we that faithful be,
And hold our craft so dear,
For 'tis our delight of a shiny night,
In the season of the year.
Oh, 'tis our delight of a shiny night,
In the season of the year.

Throughout, about and round about,
By flame that burneth bright,
We'll dance and sing, around the ring,
At witching hour of night.
Good luck to we that faithful be,
And hold our craft so dear,
For 'tis our delight of a shiny night,
In the season of the year.
Oh, 'tis our delight of a shiny night,
In the season of the year.

This is kept up until the Lady feels that it is time to stop. She then moves forward and touches East on the shoulder. He goes round once more, before breaking the circle and leading everyone out in the usual manner.

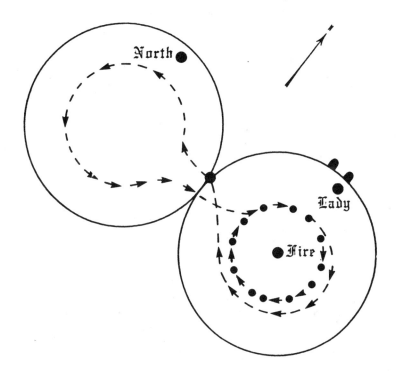

The rite ends as usual, with food and drink being brought out and everyone joining in the feast.

Hallowe'en (31 October)

For the Hallowe'en ritual the order and symbology differ greatly from those of any of the other rituals of the year. In the first instance, instead of using one circle, two are used. One circle has a fire in the centre, while the other is dark and empty.

In this ritual every member has a candle, which is carried into the circle. The Lady of the South, for this occasion, wears dark and sombre clothing. Instead of cakes and wine, cider and enough apples for each member of the group to have one are taken into the circle. The cider is taken in by the Lady of the North, while the apples are held by the Lord of the West.

Half way through the ritual, just before the coven is led off into the dark circle, North and the Lady change places. West takes up his position where the two circles join, and for this rite West takes on the attributes of Gwyn, Prince and Lord of the Mound in Celtic mythology.

The Hag, or the Lady of the North, is dressed in black, with a heavy white make-up or a white mask with blood-red lips. In this aspect she symbolizes the Pale-Faced Goddess who presides over the feast and the cauldron, in the castle that spins without motion between two worlds. (This is another concept from Celtic mythology. See *The White Goddess*, by Robert Graves.) The second circle is her domain. Here she reigns supreme, and her word is law within the circle.

The first circle is entered in the usual way, and the Lady takes up her position in the north. Once again, the rest join hands round the fire. The Lady says her particular prayer:

> Beloved Bloodmother of my especial breed,
> Welcome me at this moment with your willing womb.
> Let me learn to live in love with all you are,
> So my seeking spirit serves the Sangreal.

There is the usual pause for a few moments before the Lady goes on to say:

Lady: 'We gather this night in the darkness, for the dark is upon us. Cold is the night, and cold are our souls.'

Coven: 'We bear witness to this truth.'

Lady: 'The King is dead. The earth is awaiting the rebirth of life. At this time, we call on those who have gone before us, to join us in the dreaded circle where the Pale-Faced Goddess serves the cauldron.'

Coven: 'Thus shall we wait the call.'

Lady: 'For this is the time of mourning, the time of remembrance. The old year has passed, with all its glory. The new year is still to come. Now is the time to renew the pledge, to settle old scores, to shed the sorrows of the old year and renew the hopes for the year to come.'

Coven: 'We stand ready for to do this.'

At this point the Lady of the North breaks the circle of

hands and turns to face the Lady. At her nod, they both walk forward to change positions. On passing each other, they stop long enough for the Lady to take North's hands and touch them with her forehead, by bowing over them. The Lady takes the place of North in the circle, while North turns and faces inward.

North: 'From out of the north came the wind. Upon its breath is the chill of eternity. Within it is the call of the raven, unheard by all except those with ears attuned to listen. For it is my wind, and I have sent it forth to clear the earth of the old before the coming of the new. For I am she who waits beyond the river. To gain my halls you must enter the mound and cross the waters. There I shall greet you, teach you to look into the cauldron of yourself, and through the wisdom gained, know the path that you have placed your feet upon.'

The Lady of the North passes round the circle deosil until she reaches West. She takes him by the hand and leads him to his quarter, saying:

North: 'Come, Lord of the Mound. Prince, to thy station. Give my people light, as they cross from one reality to another.'

West: 'As you so command, Lady.'

North enters the second circle and takes up her position on the perimeter and to the north.

West lights his candle, and using this as a signal the circle is broken and the Lady leads the coven off deosil, the others forming up behind her. She makes her way to West.

West: 'What do you who stand before me, want of me?'

Lady: 'Light, to help us see beyond the veil.'

West: 'As each passes me, so light shall be given. For to see beyond the veil is one of our mysteries.'

Then as each person passes him, they bow low, and he lights their candle from his. All make their way past him and proceed to the centre of the dark circle, where they form up again. West then joins them, and everyone kneels down.

North: 'For a few moments let us pause, and think of those we loved and who have passed on. Let each of us place the candle of remembrance in the ground before us. For one day we shall want others to do likewise for us.'

Each person can, if so desired, dedicate the candle for one or more persons, using the words:

'As this light burns, so may the light of remembrance burn for [name or names], for the things that we once shared with each other and what we were to each other.'

North gives everyone a few minutes to contemplate, then gives the order to rise. Everyone does so and then, leaving the candles in the centre, they move back a few paces from the circle of light formed by them and start to tread the Mill widdershins, using the chant: 'EEE … YAH … YOH … AHH,' to call the pace. While they are doing this, North starts her own incantation:

North: 'I call on she who is as old as time, to come to me and through me enter the thoughts of those who tread the Mill. By her, for her, through her, I shall be the channel through which the wisdom of the ages shall flow to reach the minds of others. I shall carry the spark of her inspiration to these her children gathered here. For through me standing here in her name, the inspiration shall become thought, and the thought shall become word, to be passed on to those who long to hear it. For in this instant of time, I open myself to her, so that we may become as one, that the bonds between us may be strengthened and part of her wisdom passed on to us. For we are in truth hers, and children of her circle.'

The Mill is trodden until the Lady of the North feels that it is time to stop. Giving people time to get their breath back, she then calls West to her.

North: 'Prince, come forth, for it is time to give these our comrades of the circle the fruit and drink of the sacred tree.'

He goes to her, and together they consecrate the cider, using the cup and the knife in the usual way, and then the apples are dedicated.

North: 'In Our Lady's name I bid you come to me and drink, for in this cup is the symbol of the cauldron.'

The coven, led by the Lady, file past North and, after bowing their heads, are given a sip from the cup, each saying:

'In remembrance of Our Lady and the cauldron, I willingly do so.'

They then go to West, who gives them an apple each.

West: 'With this fruit come luck and good fortune for the coming year. By the eating of it, you take upon yourself that fortune the apple symbolizes. In Our Lady's name, take and eat.'

Each person returns to their place to eat the apple. While this is going on, North and West together consecrate another cup of cider, which is then poured on the ground as a libation for the shades of those departed.

North: 'In Our Lady's name, I pour this libation to the spirits of those departed, and to the Dark Guardian of the Portal.'

Coven: 'In Our Lady's name, so be it done.'

North then speaks to West again:

North: 'Prince, once more to thy station. For it is time that my people recross the river and return from whence they came.'

West returns to the place where the two circles join, while the rest of the coven pick up their candles. Any of them that are still alight are put out. When West is ready, the Lady leads the coven out of the circle and past West; each one bows to him as they pass. The coven, led by the Lady, proceeds deosil around the fire and back to their old positions. The Lady of the North is the last to leave the dark circle, pausing only to bow three times while saying:

North: 'In our Lady's name, I close this circle, and cause the circle of the dead to remain closed until the time comes round to open it again. In Our Lady's name, I do so command.'

She then returns to her station in the north and waits for the Lady to turn and face her. When she does so, the Lady speaks to North:

Lady: 'Sister, is all done and the circle closed?'

North: 'It is done, Lady, in a fit and proper manner.'

They walk towards each other. This time, North is the one to bow and touch hands with the forehead. The Lady then takes up her old position in the north, while the Lady of the North returns to her old position in the circle. The Lady closes the ritual in the usual manner, and everyone leaves the circle to form up outside it. From there they all go to the feast.

The Rite of Handfasting

With this rite there is a formal joining-together of two
people within the group. Usually this bond or contract is
celebrated between two people who have been or still are
working partners within the coven or group. The concept
of handfasting is a form of sacred marriage within the rites
and stems directly from the old forms of common law
marriage. Before the church or civil wedding became the
norm, there were many and varied ways for a couple to
declare themselves man and wife. In fact, until about the
last 250 years or so, there were very few church-contracted
marriages amongst ordinary people. As in gypsy tradition,
each area or county had its own form of civil declaration,
taken or given in public and legally recognized as a form
of marriage.

In this sense, the coven marriage or handfasting is a
mutually agreed bonding between two members of the
group or coven and is recognized by all other members of
the group as a valid and binding ceremony. At its most
limited, it is a marriage within the group and is effective
only within the group during any of the ritual meetings. In
this context, it will have no validity outside the actual
coven gathering unless the couple concerned wish it to be
carried over to the outside world.

Sometimes couples married in the eyes of Church or
State go through a handfasting as a matter of choice,
preferring to recognize the coven handfasting as the true
wedding ceremony, where both have taken their vows
before the altar stang. A member who is married but
whose spouse is not a member of the group or coven
sometimes takes a working partner as a handfast
companion within the rites. While not advocating this
idea, it must be recognized that it will arise and that to a
certain extent the membership as a whole will be involved
in the decision. To this extent, there should be – and
indeed there must be – firm rules governing this type of
handfasting, within the rules of the coven. The alternative
is to ban this sort of association all together. This too can
raise all sorts of problems within the group, as you are in
effect denying two consenting adults the right to decide

their own lives, and at the same time denying them the right to be as one within the faith. Rather than do this, it is far better to accept that people will be drawn to each other in this way. In the accepting of what after all is a fact of life, there must be certain conditions laid down to make it acceptable to the rest of the coven or group.

When two people who are married to others outside the group strongly desire to join together in a handfasting, it must be firmly understood by all concerned that:

(1) The handfasting is recognized only within the group and as such should never be carried over to the outside world; nor should it ever be used as an excuse for doing so.

(2) For the purpose of the rites, the couple are, in the eyes of the coven, considered to be husband and wife. The fact that they are not, in the context of the civil law, can have no standing. By coven rite they are joined together, and by coven rite they stay joined until they choose to dissolve the bond.

(3) The other group or coven members as such must recognize this and accept this and must accept and treat them in the same way as they would any other married couple during any of the meetings.

(4) The couple concerned must understand and accept the fact that the rite of handfasting means and stands for something within the rites and the coven and is not the same as just having an affaire. Nor should it be used as an excuse to justify an affaire. It is a solemn pledge taken by two people to hold firm to each other within the faith, and to recognize each other as a true husband or wife within the rites. If the time should come for them to dissolve the bond and separate, they should do so with no ill-feeling, and in no way bring disharmony to the group.

(5) Also, there must be the recognition that both concerned have duties and obligations to others who are outside the gathering. In this sense, any involvement within the group must be kept separate from the other life outside; and in this, care must be taken not to cause hurt to the other partner unwittingly involved. It must be remembered that, in the eyes of society, married people joining together in a handfasting outside their marriage

are committing adultery. Nothing more or less than that, no matter how the group sees it. It is this world we have to live in. So any couple who join together in a handfasting outside marriage had better be sure that they fully understand all the implications involved, and what they stand to be accused of if it is discovered or flaunted to the outside world.

On this score, I feel that any group or coven must decide for themselves as to the inclusion of the handfasting rite within their own rituals. In the case of my old group, it was done by fire and sword; and once again, this rite was peculiar to us and was ours alone.

Any group wishing to have a handfasting rite should think carefully about what is involved, and consider how they expect a couple who have been so joined to behave. Then they should create their own rite and within that ritual incorporate the pledges, promises and obligations they feel belong to the rite. When once these have been established, they should stick to them without change, and in this way create their own tradition of handfasting.

For better or for worse, this in the past was a part of the Old Religion; and as such, it is still part of the same religion today.

Appendix:
A List of Sacred Woods and Trees

With regard to the 'Nine Woods of the Beltane Fire'; ash, birch, yew, hazel, rowan, willow, pine, thorn and all other trees mentioned as being traditionally sacred may be used, with the exception of oak. This is because oak is the king of the woods. The available woods will, of course, differ in different parts of the country; the tradition is simply that the fire should consist of nine woods, with the exception of oak.

Apple: This is one of the holy trees possessing magical powers. Its fruit, when cut across, displays the magical sign of the pentagram (five-pointed star). Avalon, the old name for Glastonbury, one of Britain's most sacred centres, means 'The place of apple-trees'. At Hallowe'en a large apple, called the Allen or Hallowe'en Apple, is eaten for good luck.

Ash: This wood is used for the stang, and in this way it represents the Horned God-King. Dressed with garlands and with crossed arrows, the stang is used as an altar. In the old Norse mythology, the World-Tree was an ash, Yggdrasil, the Cosmic Axis.

Ash-Faggot: This is made up of ash twigs. It should be burned at Yule to ensure good fortune. This is the origin of the 'Yule Log'. A miniature one can be kept in the house for good luck.

Birch: This is one of the trees that is traditionally associated with the May Eve celebrations, when people used to go out overnight into the woods and bring home green boughs to decorate their homes for May Day. It is a tree of good luck and purification and as such is used in the making of the besom. It is regarded as feminine.

Blackthorn: This is an ominous tree. The blackthorn staff is sometimes used as the altar stang when a curse is being put on someone. The tree has formidable spines and is associated with the 'blackthorn winter', a time of renewed cold in the spring associated with the appearance of the blackthorn blossom.

Elder: This tree is regarded as unlucky, because of its traditional association with witchcraft. In some parts of Britain it is thought to be female. In olden days judgment was sometimes given under it. Hence the clan sword of judgment is occasionally hafted with elder wood.

Hawthorn: This is also known as the whitethorn and the maytree, because of its time-honoured association with May Day. Because it was a sacred tree, it was considered very unlucky to bring branches or flowers of the hawthorn indoors. However, if used as a decoration outdoors on May Day, it brought good luck.

Hazel: A holy tree connected with fire, fertility, knowledge, divination and poetry. The favourite wood for a water-diviner's rod. It is one of the nine sacred woods used in the Beltane fire.

Oak: The oak is the king of the woodland, especially if bearing mistletoe. Ancient oaks frequently marked a meeting-place or boundary. This is shown by the number of place-names, such as Gospel Oak, which often survive on the map even though the original tree has long gone. The oak is one of the seven 'Chieftain Trees' named in old Irish law, the unlawful felling of which was regarded as a serious crime. The other six were the hazel, apple, yew, holly, ash and pine.

Rowan: This is otherwise known as the mountain ash. Sprigs of this tree are considered to bring good luck, and to protect from black magic and the evil eye. Hence an old Celtic salutation was, 'Peace be here and rowan tree!'

Willow: This was a tree of mourning in olden days and is often referred to as such in old songs and ballads. However, its catkins gathered on May Day could be luck-bringers. It is a water-loving tree and hence traditionally associated with the influence of the moon.

Yew: This is the tree of death and resurrection. Some of the oldest yew trees are to be found in churchyards, because of this symbolism. It is a very long lived tree, and because of this and its evergreen foliage it was regarded as a symbol of immortality.

This is only a very brief sketch of tree lore. Much more may be found by study of the traditions of Britain's trees, which should cause us all to value more the woodlands, forests and hedgerows of our country.

All these trees mentioned above play a part in the rituals of the Mother Goddess, either as staffs or in the form of greenery for the garlands. The ash faggot can be made up and handed to the members at Yule, when the old faggots are burned. This, as a symbolic action, will help to strengthen the bonds of continuity in the group.

Bibliography

Frazer, Sir James, *The Golden Bough* (First published London, 1890. Many editions thereafter. Abridged edition first published 1922)

Graves, Robert, *The White Goddess* (First published Faber & Faber, London, 1946. Several subsequent editions)

Jennings, Hargrave, *The Rosicrucians: Their Rites and Mysteries* (London, 1870)

Leland, Charles Godfrey, *Aradia: or the Gospel of the Witches* (London, 1899. Reprinted by C.W. Daniel Co., London 1974 and by Samuel Weiser, New York, 1974)

Lethbridge, T.C., *Witches: Investigating an Ancient Religion* (Routledge & Kegan Paul, London, 1962)

Murray, Margaret Alice, *The Witch Cult in Western Europe* (Oxford University Press, 1921)

Murray, Margaret Alice, *The God of the Witches* (Faber & Faber, London, 1952)

Murray, Margaret Alice, *The Divine King in England* (Faber & Faber, London, 1954)

Valiente, Doreen, *Natural Magic* (Robert Hale, London, 1975)

Valiente, Doreen, *Witchcraft for Tomorrow* (Robert Hale, London, 1978)

Valiente, Doreen, *The Rebirth of Witchcraft* (Robert Hale, London, 1989)

Watkins, Alfred, *The Old Straight Track* (Methuen, London, 1926)

Here is a selection of some further books which may be found relevant and of interest.

Bord, Janet and Colin, *Earth Rites: Fertility Practices in*

Pre-Industrial Britain (Granada Publishing, St. Albans, Herts. 1982). An eye-opening survey of how many traces and relics of the Old Religion have survived into the present day.

Chamberlain, Mary, *Old Wives' Tales* (Virago Press, London, 1981). How the feminine healer began in ancient days as a priestess, and ended as a witch.

Ehrenreich, Barbara and English, Dierdre, *Witches, Midwives and Nurses* (Feminist Press, New York, 1973). How the medical profession became male-dominated, making the female healer a 'witch'.

Eisler, Riane, *The Chalice and the Blade* (Harper & Rowe, San Francisco, 1987). A detailed survey of prehistory and of the changeover from matriarchy to a male-dominated world, with its results for us all.

Farrar, Janet and Stewart, *The Witches' Way: Principles, Rituals and Beliefs of Modern Witchcraft* (Robert Hale, London, 1984). A good outline of what many present-day witches believe and practise.

Gardner, Gerald B., *Witchcraft Today* (Riders, London, 1954. Various subsequent editions). The book that started the modern witchcraft revival.

Gray, William G., *Evoking the Primal Goddess* (Llewellyn Publications, U.S.A., 1989). The latest book from the author of the 'Sangreal' rituals.

Harrison, Michael, *The Roots of Witchcraft* (Frederick Muller, London, 1973). An interesting historical account of the Old Religion.

Hitching, Francis, *Earth Magic* (Cassells, London, 1976). New ideas and discoveries about the Stone Age and its culture. Our remote ancestors can no longer be dismissed as mere savages.

L'Estrange Ewen, C., *Witch Hunting and Witch Trials* (Kegan Paul, London, 1929).

L'Estrange Ewen, C., *Witchcraft and Demonianism* (Heath Cranton, London, 1933). This book and the above are detailed historical accounts of the records of witch persecutions in England.

Matthews, John, *The Grail: Quest for the Eternal* (Thames & Hudson, London, 1981). How the concept of the Holy Grail, the 'San Greal', evolved from a pagan original.

Michell, John, *The New View Over Atlantis* (Thames & Hudson, London, 1983). Ley lines and the secrets of Britain's landscape.

Sjoo, Monica and Mor, Barbara, *The Ancient Religion of the Great Cosmic Mother of All*. (First published by Rainbow Press, Trondheim, Norway, 1981. New and enlarged edition recently published by Harper & Rowe, USA). A beautiful and moving account of the worship of the Great Goddess.

Spence, Lewis, *The Mysteries of Britain* (Riders, London, 1931). The Goddess Cerridwen and her Cauldron of Inspiration, which evolved into the Holy Grail.

Index

absent healing, 42–4
Alfriston, Sussex, 64
altar, *see* stang
altar, personal, 104–5
altar, setting up permanent, 113–14
apples, at Hallowe'en ritual, 183, 186–7
apple tree, 191
apron, Magister's, 145
Aradia, myth of, 53
Aradia: or the Gospel of the Witches, 53, 157
ash, 106, 191, *see also* stang
ash-faggot, 191, 192
Avalon, 191

banishment, 75–6
barley, ritual planting of, 158–9, 179–80
Beltane, 158
besom, 71, 84, 87, 95, 121–6
    as bridge, 123–6, 151
    nature of, 121–3
birch, 118, 123, 125, 167, 176, 191
Black, Man in, 76–7, 78
blackthorn, 102, 116, 119, 120, 191
Bran, 130

cairn, royal, 165–6, 168–70
cakes and wine, 71, 72, 105, 123

dedication of, 154–7, 177
Candlemas, 72, 73, 116, 118, 158
    ritual of, 170–6
candles, 79–80, 105, 185–6
castle, as symbol, 129
cauldron, 90, 95, 130–4, 176
Cauldron of Inspiration, 130, 153
cave paintings, 143
Celtic myths and rites, 52–3, 130, 135–6, 149
Cerridwen, 110, 130
'Chieftain trees', 192
Christianity and paganism, 24, 50, 55, 62, 112, 132, 154–5
cider, in Hallowe'en ritual, 183, 186–7
circle, casting, 88, 96–7, 104, 150–4
    twin circles, 159, 183–7
circle chant, 161–2
circle magic, 36–45
Cochrane, Robert, 13–14, 28, 31, 149
consecration of tools, 107–9, 115
Constantinople, Council of (484), 50
cord, 95, 99–102
    colours of, 99
    in consecration of stang, 108
    exchange of, 99, 102
    knots in, 99–100, 102

symbolic meaning, 100–6
cornstalk, cutting of, 72, 158–9, 179–80
coven
  membership of, 71–8
  setting up, 73
coven names, 74
coven tools, 110–45
cup, 95, 110–12
cursing, 41, 44–5, 116, 119–20

Diana, 53–4, 59–60, 104, 116
  sacred grove of, 106
disorientation of body, 161
divination, 34–5, 130
Divine King, 26, 49, 58, 62, 66, 101, 112, 113, 144–5, 154, 166–9 see also Horned King
Dodmen, 103
dormant facilities, using, 34–6
Drawing Down the Power, 155
dream recall, 31

East, Officer of the, 72
  appropriate cord, 99
  role in Candlemas rite, 173–6
  role in casting the circle, 151–2
  role in cursing, 128
  role in Lammas rite, 181
  role in May Eve Rite, 177–8
  role in oath of initiation, 79–81
  role in oath of membership, 81, 83
  role in oath of office, 84
  role in oath-taking of Lady, 87, 88–91
  use of besom, 123
  use of knife, 114
Easter, 159–60
Edward III, King, 55

elder, 129–30, 191
elements, 108, 137, 140
equinoxes, 159
Eucharist, 154–5
evil spirits, conjuration of, 39–40
Ewen, C.L'Estrange, 56n
expulsion, 75–6

fasting, 160–1
fire, lighting the, 151
  woods to be used, 191–2
Frazer, Sir James, The Golden Bough, 58

garlands, 118–19
garotte, used in sacrifice, 100–1
Goodfellow, Robin, 63, 104
Graves, Robert, The White Goddess, 184
Green Man, the, 63–4
guardian spirits, animals as, 24, 47
Gwynn ap Nudd, 73, 153, 184

Hag, 42, 54, 72, 101, 184
Hallowe'en, 72, 73, 79, 118–19, 159
  ritual of, 183–7
handfasting, 188–90
hawthorn, 118, 176, 191–2
hazel, 118, 123, 125, 192
healing, art of, 41–4, 57, 65
  absent healing, 42–4
  by coven, 42–4
  by individual, 42
Heb-Seb ceremony, Egypt, 166
Hecate, 54
herbal lore, 41–2, 57, 65
Herne the Hunter, 59, 73, 116–17, 120, 153
Holy Grail, 26, 111, 112, 133
Hood, Robin, 63–6, 104

Horned God, 23, 54–67 *passim*, 106, 117, 120, 144, 145, 153
Horned King, 51, 58, 67, 145, 158, 165, *see also* Divine King
Hounds of Hell, 73, 116

initiates, 74–6
  appropriate cord, 99
  breaking an oath, 75
  leaving a coven, 75
initiation, oath of, 79–81
initiation period, 27–8
Inner Plane contact, 87
iron, 121

Jack-in-the-Green, 49, 103
Jennings, Hargrave, *The Rosicrucians: Their Rites and Mysteries*, 131
Joan of Arc, 55

Kent, Fair Maid of, 55
knife, 95
  cleansing, 97–8
  consecration of, 97–8, 107–9
  sacred nature of, 98
  symbolism of, 96, 112, 114
  uses of, 96–8
knife, coven, 113–15
  consecration of, 115
  substitute for sword, 115
  used in casting circle, 151

Lady, The, 59, 71–2, 76, 123
  appropriate cord, 99
  role in Candlemas rite, 170–6
  role in casting the circle, 151–3
  role in Hallowe'en rite, 184–7
  role in oath of initiation, 80–1
  role in oath of membership, 81–3
  role in oath of office, 84–7
  role in rite of purification, 164–5
  role in skull naming, 141
  taking up office, 87–94
  tokens of office, 88, 89
Lammas, 118, 158–9
  ritual of, 179–83
  'Lammas Growth,' 159
Leland, Charles Godfrey, *Aradia: or the Gospel of the Witches*, 53, 157
Lethbridge, T.C., *Witches: Investigating an Ancient Religion*, 162
Llantilio Crossenny, Monmouthshire, 63

magic, concept of, 33–4
magic of circle, 36–45
magic of self, 34–6
Magister, 59, 122, 145
manifestations, physical, 38–40
Marian, Maid, 65
marriage rites, 188–90
May Eve, 59, 103, 113, 118, 131, 158, 166, 191
  rite of, 176–9
'Men of the Leys', 103
Middle Ages, Witchcraft in, 55–8, 62–8
Midsummer, solstice of, 159
Midwinter, solstice of, 159
Milan, Edict of (313), 50
Misrule, Lord of, 58
moon,
  aspects of, 43–4, 48
  phases of, 107
Mound, Lord of the, 73
Murray, Dr Margaret, 55

Nicaea, Council of (325), 50

North, Lady of the, 72, 101
  appropriate cord, 99
  role in Hallowe'en ritual, 183–7
  role in oath-taking of Lady, 88, 89
Norwich Cathedral, 63
nude, working in, 104

oak, 116–17, 159, 192
oath-taking, 72, 74, 76
  changing of cords at, 99
  oath for the Lady, 87–91
  oath of initiation, 79–81
  oath of membership, 81–3, 100, 102
  oath of office, 83–87
office, standing for, 83–4
overlooking, 35–6

Pale-Faced Goddess, 72, 101, 130, 184
Peasants' Revolt (1381), 61–2
peat bogs, bodies discovered in, 100–1
Plantagenets, 62
phallic symbolism, 96, 112, 114, 122–3
precognition, 34
priest kings, 54–5, 103
purification, rite of, 45, 163–5

Rais, Gilles de, 55
records, keeping, 72, 77
relics, holy, 135
Richard II, King, 61–2
Roman Empire, 50
rose symbol, 129
Rosslyn Chapel, Edinburgh, 64
rowan, 192

Sabbats, Great, 158–9, 160
Sabbats, Lesser, 159–60

sacrifice, animal, 54, 59, 142–5
sacrifice, human, 49, 54, 100–1
  of Divine King, 58, 101, 112, 113, 144–5
sacrificial scapegoat, 144–5
Samhain Eve, 159
Sangreal, 112
Sangreal Prayer, 26, 81, 83, 84, 90, 109, 176–7, 180, 184
Saturnalia, 58
scapegoat, 144–5
scrying, 133
seven-year reign, tradition of, 59, 145, 166
severed head, cult of, 135
sex magic, 122
skull, mythos of, 40, 134–45
  cleansing and purification, 137, 139–40
  functions of, 142–5
  introduction of, 138
  naming of, 138, 141
  in prophecy, 142–3
  as totem, 143–5
smithcraft, 121
solstices, 159
soul candle, 79–80
South, Lady of the, 72
  appropriate cord, 99
  role in Hallowe'en rite, 183
  role in Lammas rite, 179–81
  role in membership oath, 82–3, 100, 102
  role in oath-taking of Lady, 89
Spence, Lewis, *The Mysteries of Britain*, 111
spirits, contact with, 39–40, 137–9, 143
spontaneous contact, 37–8
spontaneous manifestations, 38–40
stang, 23, 59–60, 95, 102–7,

116–21, 145
consecrating, 106, 108–9
coven, 116–21
cutting, 97, 106
garlanding, 118–19
personal, 102–7, 108–9
shodding, 106, 121
symbolism of, 103–4, 145
Summers, Montague, 56n
Summoner, The, 77–8
sword, 81–95 *passim*, 126–30
forging, 128–9
for justice, 127
haft, 129–30
use in banishing, 127–8
use in cursing, 127, 128
use in oath-taking, 127
sympathetic magic, 143

telepathy, 34
tools, 95–109, 110–45
coven, 95, 110–45
personal, 95, 96–109
totems, animal, 24, 47, 59, 120–1
transubstantiation, 155

Undry, 130
Ur, Royal Cemetery at, 100

Valiente, Doreen
Natural Magic, 33

Witchcraft for Tomorrow, 182
Vespasian, Temple of, Rome, 113

Walpurgis Night, 158
Watkins, Alfred, *The Old Straight Track*, 103
West, Officer of the, 73
appropriate cord, 99
role in Hallowe'en rite, 183–7
role in oath-taking of Lady, 89, 90
role in rite of purification, 164–5
wheat, ritual planting of, 158–9, 179–80
Wild Hunt, 59, 73, 116, 153, 158, 170
William Rufus, King, 55, 159
willow, 118, 176, 192
Windsor Great Park, 116–17
wine, 72, 105, 123
consecration of, 96, 111–12, 154–7
witchcraft, hierarchical systems in, 28
witch trials, 56–7, 62–3

yew, 123, 125, 128, 192
Yggdrasil, 191
Yule, 119, 159